SIGNATURE KNITS

SIGNATURE KNITS

KNITS

A Designer's Portfolio
of Create-Your-Own Classics

GLENORA KELLY SMITH

Photographs by Jeffrey Hackett
Illustrations by Mary Walsh

CHARLES SCRIBNER'S SONS   NEW YORK

ACKNOWLEDGMENTS

A very special thanks to those who so intimately shared the birth of a book, especially:

To Jeff, for his patience and precision in capturing the creativity . . . a superb photographer.

To Mary, for her insight and imagination in drawing the designs . . . a very talented artist.

Library of Congress Cataloging-in-Publication Data

Smith, Glenora Kelly.
   Signature knits.
   Bibliography: p.
   1. Knitting—Patterns. I. Title.
TT820.S544   1986   746.9′2   85–30299
ISBN 0-684-18473-7

1 3 5 7 9 11 13 15 17 19 Q C 20 18 16 14 12 10 8 6 4 2

Printed in the United States of America.

*When you sit in the silence
and listen to your soul,
     time is timeless
     place becomes space,
          and the music that you hear
          grows from within
          and echoes around
          the lives you hold most dear...*

*For my children, Glenora and Chad,
For my Mother and Dad
whose worlds I lovingly share...
and for friends, who care!*

Contents

Introduction

In *Signature Knits* I present a portfolio of original create-your-own classics, designed to offer you several unique features:

Projects on three different *dexterity* levels
Variety of natural and novelty *fibers*
Mixture of neutral, pastel, and vibrant *colors*
Mixed media, "picture," and "patchwork" *effects*
Feather, fur, organdy, and antique *trims*
Designs with embroidery and crochet *embellishments*
Dual instruction for some designs *(hand* and *machine)*
An exciting collection of *accessories*
Designs for *simple stitchery* with *finesse*

The instructions are meant to make everyone, especially beginners, feel at ease. **There are no abbreviations.** Simple stitchery, based on garter (knit every row) or stockinette (knit 1 row, purl 1 row), is used for many designs. Other designs offer a variety of stitchery to expand your knowledge and let you explore intermediate and advanced levels of complexity. There are also several choices offered for decorative trims and fashionable finishes. The same design may be knit in a sporty or dressy fiber, plain or patterned stitch, pale or bold color; it may be untrimmed or embellished with beads, flowers, or feathers. The designs are classic, always in style. Your signature touches will make your own distinctive design statement. The creative options are endless—so enjoy!

Fashion Flair

Being fashionable is *not* following the latest fads or styles, as many people think. It is being aware of the fashions of the times and adapting them to suit your own personality, color preferences, and most flattering silhouettes.

Someone with a flair for fashion is aware of herself and is secure in her choices. Fashion is as diverse as the people who design it and the people who wear it. It can be beautifully elegant, a quiet understatement of subtle sophistication, a refinement of your taste. Or it can be outrageously flamboyant and fun, a whimsical and amusing expression of yourself. Defining yourself is the key to developing fashion flair. Self-awareness frees you from following the current trend. With confidence, you can develop your own style and design the clothes that express it best.

The fashions we call classic are those that have withstood the test of time and will continue to do so. They are the backbone of the fashion world. Classics reflect a strength, often in simplicity of line, that stands on its own, as in painting and sculpture. Classics are far from plain, for within and around them are trends that come and go, some faster than others, that reflect the moods and activities of the time. Many of these fashion fads are cycles that repeat themselves many times over, but always return with a new twist, a freshness and vitality that spark a new beginning. They flash before us, adding adventurous flavor to the fashion world, and expose us to new ideas, new techniques, new decorations—a refreshing new outlook on ourselves. Above all else, fashion should be fun.

WHAT IS A PORTFOLIO?

A designer's portfolio represents the best of his or her work, culled over a period of time from a myriad of explorations into the elements of design. Here lines and spaces, colors and textures, contours and contrasts have all been structured to create each design. It is from this very structure that your own signature will evolve, for knowledge of the mechanics helps you produce the design you visualize. You, as designer, balance and mix the elements, defining your personal style.

ELEMENTS OF DESIGN

The basic elements of design are *structural* and *visual*. The structural elements are the essential parts, the framework of the design—the parts that "hold it together." They organize and define a design. The visual elements are those we actually see: the expressive, creative, imaginative ingredients of a design. We appreciate the visual and artistic elements of design in a physical and emotional as well as an intellectual manner.

There are certain principles that apply to any type of design. *Line* and *space* are basic elements. Lines serve to define and support space; they are the framework on which it hangs or flows freely. Lines are the dimensions and directions in which the space moves. Lines, whether straight or curved, are the most vital forms of visual expression known. Line defines shape, be it geometric, abstract, natural, or illusory. Space, in and of itself, defined or undefined, suspended or stabilized, becomes an intrinsic part of an overall design. Space can be a focal point or background, a small or large proportion, a closed and static element or an open and flowing catalyst. The relationship of spaces defines the scale of your design.

Color and *contrast* are the playful elements of design. They are constantly in motion, for every color becomes a different one when placed next to another. Color is a force based on similarities and contrasts. Color preferences are very personal. The best guide you have to color choices is knowing yourself. In designing, forget color fads; they pass very quickly. Your personal preferences are bound to grow and change, but they are yours alone, an intrinsic part of your signature.

The differences between light and dark tones allow us to see form. The stronger the contrast, the stronger the form. Contrast is created by the intensity or dullness, lightness or darkness, shade or hue of a particular color, all of which are influenced by *texture* and *tone,* the sensual element of a design. Design is most often thought of in its tactile state: Is the texture rough or smooth? However, the more subtle factors of dullness or shine are visual textures; hence the same color may appear as two distinct colors but be merely two different textures.

Harmony and *balance* compose good design. The potentials and limitations of space, the positions of shapes and forms, the diversity of textures, as well as the intensity and values of colors, are all part of the plan. The interplay of structural and visual elements creates the harmony and balance.

In each Signature Knit all the structural and visual principles are apparent: line and space, color and contrast, texture and tone. However, each of us sees a design differently because everyone's taste varies. These design principles become the filters for your personal fashion flair. Some people enjoy bold lines, bright colors, and strong statements such as those you see in the Toga and the Stained-Glass Camisole. Some prefer a subtle interplay of textures and soft tones, as seen in Sunrise Scoop and Mixed Media Scoop or Cloud Camisole. Still others tend toward an understatement of quiet elegance, as echoed in Silk Ombré or Ruffled Wrap. Moods and seasons as well as special occasions help you make your choices.

Fibers

Fibers are fabulous! There are a staggering number of them, and their colors are incredible. The qualities and characteristics of fibers form an integral part of a design. Often, distinctive features of the fiber will suggest a design. By its very nature a tweedy, heavy-textured yarn lends itself to a sporty design. A light, fluffy, delicate fiber lends itself to an elegant evening design.

There are two classes of fiber: natural and synthetic.

NATURAL FIBERS

Natural fibers are derived from plant or animal sources. These fibers vary greatly in weight, ply, and texture and react beautifully to dyes. Wool, silk, cotton, and linen are natural fibers.

Wool

Wool is derived from the fine, soft hair that forms the fleece on domestic sheep. In general, wools have a wonderful depth and strength within the fibers themselves. A sheep farmer may inform you that truly fine wool fiber will stretch one-third its length and is four times stronger than cotton. Wool provides a great deal of natural warmth, for it traps air within the fibers, which then acts as insulation, holding in body warmth. It has exceptional absorbency but weakens and stretches when wet. Wool fibers must be classified and labeled according to their origin: virgin wool—has never been used; pure wool—may contain only 5 percent of another fiber; reprocessed wool—recycled fiber. Wool has limited resistance to abrasion and is likely to pill or shrink if not treated properly.

Knitting worsted is a 4-ply yarn of heavy weight, suitable for warm sweaters and outdoor wear—mittens, gloves, and hats. *Sport yarn* is also a 4-ply worsted yarn but is finer in bulk, lighter in weight, and suitable for overall sportswear designs.

Silk

Silk is made from the cocoon of the silk worm. The cocoon itself is actually unrolled in one continuous filament; this is spun into fine, lustrous threads to create silk yarn—resilient, light, and strong. Soft and simply scrumptious, silk has excellent wrinkle, mildew, and moth resistance and is a very absorbent fiber as well. In fact, it is the favorite of hand dyers, for it has a superb affinity for dyes and lends itself to subtle shadings and ombré effects, although it may have a tendency to bleed. Check your sample swatch before beginning the project.

Silk ribbon, made in Japan, is a treat for your fingers and a feast for your eyes. It is flat rather than round, thin and smooth, like silk fabric, with the same sheen and depth to the colors—precious indeed.

Silk twist is a 2-ply fiber, tightly twisted in the same manner and weight as perle cotton. Hand-dyed silk twist is by far the most exquisite silk and the most expensive fiber, but well worth it. The silk fiber's natural striations and shadings are still apparent after dying, resulting in a subtle sophistication in even the simplest design. Working with silk twist is like working with butter. A word of warning: Silk twist tends to stretch, so rewind it by hand *very tightly* before working.

Silk bouclé has a softer feel than twist, for the loose, loopy strands, which are not twisted, accentuate the natural softness of silk fibers. It is often combined with a cotton or synthetic core for strength and stability (the core controls stretch).

Cotton

Cotton is the soft, fluffy white substance derived from the cotton plant, and the term refers to all its derivatives: thread, yarn, and fabric. Cotton has been spun, dyed, and woven since prehistoric times, for it is the fiber from which clothing was made in ancient India, Egypt, and China. Cotton fabrics found in Peruvian tombs are believed to date from a pre-Incan culture. The plant itself is of tropical origin and is related to the hibiscus and hollyhock. The ripe cotton is plucked from the seeds and dried, then flattened and twisted. The fibers are cream- or buff-colored and must be bleached to become white.

Cotton is extremely versatile and varies in weight and texture. It is very strong but does have a tendency to wrinkle. Comfortable and absorbent, it dyes easily but will shrink a great deal unless treated prior to use. Unlike wool, which acts as an insulator, cotton has a tendency to draw the heat away from the body, making it a very popular fiber in warm climates.

Cotton embroidery floss has 6 threads of mercerized cotton per strand. It is a thin, smooth, very fine yarn with such a beautiful luster that it is often mistaken for silk. The color range is vast.

Perle cotton is a mercerized cotton yarn; 2 plies are twisted to form a strand. It is very shiny and smooth and is available in several weights and a wide range of pastel and bright colors.

Cotton bouclé is made of several twisted threads, with one or two of them left untwisted (loose and loopy) at intervals. This gives the yarn a nubby texture, although it is soft to the touch. It is available in several weights, with a dull or glossy finish, and in a wide range of colors. A popular choice is a bouclé with several colors spun within the same strand for some exciting interaction in the fiber itself.

Crochet cotton is a smooth, low-luster cotton, cabled rather than twisted so it will not crimp or buckle when used for crochet. It is becoming popular for knitting as well because of its ease in handling, variety of colors and weights, economy, and seasonal comfort.

Linen

Linen, a fiber made from linen flax, is derived from the stem of the blue-flowered linseed plant. Since its natural fibers are a pale yellow when processed, the colors are often soft and subtle.

Linen is available in different weights, from very fine yarn to heavy, nubby yarn. It has a very soft natural luster that sometimes makes it difficult to dye; deep colors may bleed. It will wrinkle and shrink easily unless the fibers are pretreated. Linen is unusually strong but stiff and tends to wear where it is creased. However, it has been considered one of the elegant fibers for some time and continues to be in the fashion world.

European linen is a very fine 2-ply yarn of excellent quality with a slight sheen. The colors are primarily the pastel and muted tones found in European tapestry and embroidery. The results are exceptional, with soft but full-bodied garments that have subtle striations in the color.

Domestic linen is made from a cruder flax than the European linen. It tends to have numerous slubs and a different finish. It is usually found in a heavier weight and looks far less refined when knit.

SYNTHETIC FIBERS

Synthetics (or artificial fibers—the terms are often used synonymously) are fibers manufactured through a synthesis (a combining of elements). Synthetics are being discovered every day, some from natural sources, such as cellulose or protein, others from chemical origins.

Acetate fibers have a very shiny, silklike appearance. They are often blended with other fibers because they drape well, but they have a tendency to wrinkle and give off a great deal of static. Acetate resists stretching or shrinking; however, it is not a strong fiber and becomes even weaker when exposed to light.

Rayon, a synthetic fiber made from cellulose, has a dubious reputation, for it was one of the early man-made fibers and the range of quality is wide. A type of acetate, it has relatively low strength and wrinkles easily. It has a tendency to shrink when laundered, as well as stretch completely out of shape when worn unless the fiber has been carefully treated. In general, an inexpensive rayon yarn will *not* be a bargain.

Rayon is exceedingly glossy, almost glasslike, and very slippery, making it somewhat difficult to work. Some varieties are exceptionally springy, and it is a challenge to keep your handwork under control. It is most often combined with other fibers for an interesting textural effect. The colors are vibrant and strong.

Modacrylics are primarily deep-piled fibers, such as chenille or simulated fur. Most often found in blends, they retain their shape well and have a great deal of elasticity, making them popular for trims.

Metallics are generally made of aluminized polyester film. These are coated, then dyed and slit into lengths, and processed into various types of yarn—flat, twisted, braided, or crocheted—to create an endless variety of fibers. True metal yarns are made from actual flat or round metal wire wound around a core. Blending metallic filaments are very fine and used with other fibers for accents and highlights.

Synthetic *ribbon* is a marvelous maverick. It has the same characteristics as its silk counterpart. It is a narrow band of fine filaments woven into long strips resembling silk fabric but not as soft. Its economic advantage has led many to appreciate the unique results of ribbon.

Chenille is a yarn with a long, velvety pile. Although once made of cotton, it is now made primarily from fluffy acrylic fibers spun around a rayon core. The length and tightness of the pile determine the weight of the chenille. A quality fiber is lustrous, full-bodied, and soft, with a rich, velvet impression when worked.

Knitting worsted and *sport yarn* also come in their synthetic derivatives, allowing for easier handling and maintenance.

SENSATIONAL FIBERS

Sensational seems to be the direction in which fibers are running. Anything that you can bend, weave, twist, or coerce into being a fiber becomes one, whether it's flat, round, lumpy, or otherwise a tube, strip, or ribbon. The spectrum is infinite, limited only by your imagination.

Angora and *mohair* are made from the long, silky hair of the Angora rabbit or Angora goat. The rabbits have been bred primarily for this specific purpose. However, the goats have been used for centuries and are now being bred in the United States and South Africa. Usually angora and mohair are 2- or 3-ply yarns with brushed fibers wound around a central core to create a fluffy effect. These fibers are often combined with wool, silk, or cotton. Synthetic mohair is also found on the market.

Feathers and *fur* are fast becoming recognized as fashion fibers, whether spun in with other fibers to create a yarn or couched, woven, or actually knit in strips. Primarily used as trims and accents, some can be worked within the design itself. Among the feathers are turkey, marabou, ostrich, cock, and pheasant.

Leather and *suede* are also available now in various ribbon-like strips with a variety of textures—flat, embossed, shiny, dull, some simulating reptile and snake skin. The colors reflect the natural tones of the skins, but new tones, particularly in the suedes and pseudo-suedes, are now available (some are even two-tone).

Numerous *novelty yarns* are appearing on the market at an incredible pace. Some are often simply redefinitions of a fiber forgotten or used in a mundane manner; for example, the nylon organdy ribbon now sold in spools is none other than a re-vamping of the old seam binding so popular in commercial knitwear. However, in the hands of a creative craftsperson, its opulence and fluidity become very exciting indeed.

Many fiber artists are creating their own novelty fibers for their handwork, and some are too marvelous not to market. Some curious, some creative, all contribute in their unique way to those of us who consider ourselves thread benders. Strips of *raw-edged fabrics*—prints or solids, cottons and wools, thick and thin—which have been widely used among weavers, are now finding their way into the fingers of other crafts people. Metallic, cotton, and acrylic *fringes*, otherwise considered trims, are now becoming an integral part of textile designs. Other members of the "notions" department are weaving their way into the fiber world. *Soutache braid, rayon rattail,* and

MAJOR FIBER CATEGORIES

Wool	Silk	Cotton	Linen	Synthetics	Sensational
Worsted	Ribbon	Floss	European	Acetate	Angora,
Sport	Twist	Perle	Domestic	Rayon	mohair
	Bouclé	Bouclé		Modacrylics	Feathers,
		Crochet		Metallics	fur
				Ribbon	Leather,
				Chenille	suede
					Novelty

YARN VOCABULARY

Thread:	A filament or fiber from which yarn is made
Yarn:	Any spun thread
Strand:	A single length of thread or yarn
Ply:	The number of twisted threads in one strand of yarn
Skein:	A small coiled bundle of thread or yarn. Various yardages and weights can equal one skein
Mercerized:	A treatment (under tension) with caustic soda to give cotton yarn a receptiveness to dye and add luster and strength

chained and cabled *cording* are among them. The bright, vibrant colors make them dramatic; many are intertwined with metallics, making them all the more novel.

CARE AND FEEDING OF FIBERS

The best advice on caring for any fiber is simply "tender, loving care"—and all the more so when you have spent your time and talent in creating something special. The wisest overall rule is to follow the manufacturer's instructions, usually found on the yarn label. If there are none, write the manufacturer and inquire about the yarn, for there are so many yarns on the market today made from various combinations of fibers. If you still have questions, the safest method is to gently hand-wash in cold water with a mild soap manufactured for that purpose. Never hang a knit to dry, but roll it in a towel to absorb excess moisture, lay it flat, and reshape it. Allow it to dry in a cool, airy place, not near a heat source or in the sun, which may shrink or fade the fibers.

DYE LOTS

Be sure to purchase enough yarn, all from the same dye lot, at the beginning of your project, because there is frequently a major difference from dye lot to dye lot, even in the same color, which can show dramatically in your work. Some shops are willing to hold extra yarn for you while you work your project. Should you unwittingly create a disaster, the demarcation or lines made by differences in dye lots may be disguised by the addition of a stripe or zigzag pattern to your design. Unfortunately, however, you often discover the disaster after the fact, for a very subtle difference in dye lot may not be apparent until you have finished your project. Don't panic! Simply embellish your work with embroidery or a duplicate stitch (see "Embroidery") in another color. You can also couch or weave other yarns, as well as work appliqué or novelty trims into the design.

THOUGHTS ON DYEING FIBERS

It seems to me that there are two kinds of fiber people. There are those of us who buy something lovely when we see it, and will have it about until inspiration strikes, and play with combinations (for hours), and those who plan the project first, and then buy the materials. Jasper Johns puts it another way: "Sometimes I see it and then paint it. Other times I paint it and then see it."

I love choices. Customers often get "mad" at me because the choices are so difficult. We love the different combinations for different reasons. But at the dye pot there are the same decisions to be made. I suffer from the same dilemma as the customer, and have no restraint; I've got to see all those combinations/alternatives on my bouclés, chenilles, flakes, nubs, cords, hairs, ribbons, handspuns, homespuns, feathers, and fabrics.

I love my hand-dyed colors. I dye for a living because I am seduced by monochromes, subtle gradations, furtive shades, confetti, rich vibrance, veiled shades, almost no color, muddies, colors pure and simple, uncensored, uncluttered, unexpected, flat, matte, shiny, crystal, exuberant, flamboyant, influencing, and infinite.

—Laurel Sanford Scheeler (The Sheepish Grin)

METRICS/COMMON WEIGHTS AND MEASURES EQUIVALENTS

Ounces to Grams			*Grams to Ounces*		
1	=	28.4	25	=	⅞
2	=	56.7	40	=	1⅖
3	=	85.0	50	=	1¾
4	=	113.4	100	=	3½
Yards to Meters			*Meters to Yards*		
1	=	.91	1	=	1.094
10	=	9.14	25	=	27.34
50	=	45.5	50	=	54.68
75	=	68.25	75	=	82.02
100	=	91.44	100	=	109.36

Creating Your Own Designs

BEGINNING TECHNIQUES

Discover new designs. Don't feel you have to copy other people's designs, even those in this book. Take one section of a design and replace it with a bold color or novelty fiber. Turn the design sideways or upside down. Play with it until you are happy with it and will want to spend the time and talent to actually create it. Never feel locked into a design, for things begin to happen as you work. I suggest you start with a plan in mind and head in a particular direction, but remember that side roads are often the preferred route.

To get the full effect, work your design in scale on graph paper with colored pencils. Lay the strands of yarn over your drawing to see the subtle interplay of texture. Look at it in daylight and artificial light for a realistic evaluation of its impact.

Don't limit your ideas to your yarn basket—after all, yarn is composed of fibers, and fibers are all around us. Don't overlook some corners you might ordinarily ignore such as the linen line in your son's tackle box or your daughter's discarded hair ribbons. Explore all the exciting leftovers from other projects.

There are a few general rules that keep scraps from looking like the remains of a cat fight. Choose one ingredient as a catalyst, to make it all work, to hold it all together. It can be a theme or a color—a single one or a repeated rhythm of colors. It can be a texture or series of shapes. With the purchase of a few skeins of yarn, you can harmonize several scraps that would otherwise simply be haphazard.

YOUR SIGNATURE

Here's how to use this chart. Just decide on a particular silhouette. Then choose a stitch for the edges and a stitch for the bodice. Work a sample swatch, compare it with the pattern requirements, and adjust accordingly. You then have options for a neckline, perhaps using the front from one pattern and the back from another pattern. Your next choice is with sleeves or without, then your personal preference for embellishments or not. You may decide that the fiber and design speak for themselves. This process is meant to be a continuous feast—so do come back for more!

BUILDING YOUR SIGNATURE SILHOUETTE

Edges	Bodice	Neckline	Sleeves	Embellishments
ribbing (k1, p1)	stockinette	crew	sleeveless	feathers: marabou, turkey, pheasant, ostrich
moss stitch	reverse stockinette	bateau	cap sleeve	antique finds: buttons, bows, buckles, lace, tassels
				fur scraps: sable, beaver
chevron	garter	U neck	short puff	beads: glass, pewter, crystal
single crochet	shell stitch	scoop	long narrow	fabric sleeves: chiffon, lace, net
shell crochet	fan stitch	V neck		embroidery, needlepoint
knitting spool		low back		unique fibers: organdy, metallics, bouclé
		halter		crochet: flower, leaves, butterfly
		bandeau		fabric and ribbon: flowers, ruffles
		toga		curiosities: dried flowers, shells

BEFORE YOU START:
NOTES ON INSTRUCTIONS

Here are some helpful notes on terminology. For further instructional notes, see "Basic Stitchery."

Asterisk   A reference to a drawing accompanying the instructions.

Center Front or Back   Varies with each person's size and shape. It is therefore more accurate to use the following method rather than a specific number of stitches, which might not apply to every situation. Count the number of stitches that comprise the front or back (e.g., 50); divide this number in half to find the center front (e.g., 25); place marker; count the number of stitches to bind off (e.g., 10); divide this number in half (e.g., 5); place marker on each side of center point; bind off stitches in between markers, or work instructions accordingly (sometimes working one half, then the other half, sometimes decreasing from center point).

Circular Needle   A needle with a flexible wire or plastic tube at the center and a standard needle point at either end. It is important to choose the correct length, for a needle too long will stretch the stitches, and thus the garment, out of shape. You tie the ends of the cast-on row together and knit in the round; thus, if you don't want to purl, you can still create a stockinette stitch. It also enables you to avoid side seams, as the garment is knit in a tube.

Decrease   Combining several stitches to make 1 stitch, which results in a narrowing of the design.

E-Wrap   Take the yarn and make a cursive "e," as in script, around each needle of the knitting machine.

Gauge   Refers to the number of stitches and number of rows per inch. The size of the needle and density of the yarn determine the gauge. Stitches are measured horizontally; rows are measured vertically. The instructions for each design pertain to a specific gauge for that particular design and fiber.

Increase   Working 2 or more stitches from 1 stitch, which results in a widening of the design.

Knit   The yarn is worked behind the stitch, and interlocking loops are formed to create a knitted fabric.

Main Yarn   Yarn used for the design you are working on the knitting machine.

Multiple   Refers to the number of stitches used for a specific pattern. Hence, if your pattern requires 6 stitches, you cast on in multiples of 6. If your gauge requires more or less stitches —e.g., 52 stitches— then you add or subtract accordingly (+2 on either side), thereby centering your pattern.

Parentheses   The medium- and large-size instructions are given in parentheses following the small-size instructions.

Ply   The number of twisted fibers in a single strand of yarn. The number of ply does not necessarily relate to the thickness of the yarn. Some very fine silk or baby yarns are 6- or 3-ply, and some bulky yarns are a single ply of thick and thin spun as a single strand.

Purl   The yarn is worked in front of the stitch, producing a ridged or wavy pattern in the fabric.

Rip Out   Is no fun but does make you feel better when the design looks great upon completion! To rip out, remove your work from the needles and gently pull out the strand of yarn you have been working with, unraveling the stitchery to the desired place. Correct your mistake and replace the stitches on the needle, being sure they are replaced in their original position.

Selvage   Refers to the finished edge of the work (straight or shaped). It does not refer to the edges, trims, or rib itself.

Skein (or Hank)   A coiled length of fiber that can be of any weight, length, or amount. It is *not* a measurement.

Swatch   A small sample, 4″ square, worked in the yarn and pattern stitch you choose for your design, with the suggested needle size. This swatch gives you the gauge and thus ensures the proper fit. Another important reason for making a test swatch is to get the feel of the particular fiber you have chosen. *It is of utmost importance to work a test swatch.* (See also "Size and Shape.")

Tails   The loose ends of the yarn where you stop or start work. These should be carefully woven into the back of your design to avoid unraveling.

Tension   The resistance of the yarn as it passes through your fingers. A moderate tension is best—too loose, and your stitches become uneven, making your garment sag; too tight, and your stitches become lumpy and the garment does not fit. Everyone's tension varies, which is why a test swatch is vital. A consistent tension is the important factor, and once you are comfortable with the fiber you are working, you will develop a natural rhythm and consistent tension.

Waste Yarn   Surplus yarn used to start and finish the first few inches of machine knitting.

Work Evenly   Continue to work the stitchery without increasing or decreasing stitches.

SIZE AND SHAPE

If you want your garment to fit you, follow the one cardinal rule of knitting: *Make a test swatch.* Instructions are only a tool. You are the craftsperson. Just as everyone's handwriting is different, everyone's handwork varies. Every fiber has its peculiarities. A swatch gives you a capsule view of your project: the textural results of the fiber, as well as the visual results of the stitchery itself. *Now* is the time to experiment and make changes. It is also the time to measure. Your gauge is the key to your success—and thus your enjoyment of knitting. The gauge refers to the number of stitches and number of rows per inch. Measure carefully. A piece of about 20 to 30 stitches, worked in the design stitch for 3″ to 4″, is necessary for a swatch. The thicker the yarn, the easier it is to err. Measure the stitches and rows in the center of the swatch where tension is likely to be even. Don't forget to count half stitches, for they add up to inches at the end of a row—a fit or misfit!

To determine size, measure yourself at the fullest part of the waist and bust. Size small (dress size 8–10) is for someone who measures 25″ in the waist and 32½″ in the bust; size medium (dress size 10–12): waist measures 26½″, bust measures 34″; size large (dress size 12–14): waist measures 28″, bust measures from 36″. If you are petite or extralarge, the ratio found within the instructions—5 stitches variable, ½ inch variable—can simply be subtracted or added at the proper point in the instructions.

Keep in mind that the type of yarn affects the fit. A bulky knit, in general, fits more loosely than a garment made with finer yarn. Personal preference is the key, as well as the sportiness or dressiness of the garment.

HOW TO TAKE MEASUREMENTS

Shoulders	Width is across the back along the edges of the shoulder bones. Length is from the base of the neck to the tip of the shoulder.
Waist	Found where your body naturally indents.
Hips	Must be measured around the fullest part.
Bust	Measure around fullest portion of bust, including the back.
Wrist	Just above the wristbone.
Sleeve Length	Measure at the underarm seam, 1″ below your armpit, to wrist.
Bodice Length	Measure from center of shoulder "seam" to your natural waistline.

BASIC EQUIPMENT

Here's a checklist of accessories that come in handy when you're working these designs.

Bobbins   Come in numerous shapes and sizes and are used for winding portions of yarn when separate yarns are needed for working an area. When starting a new design area, be sure to wrap new bobbin around previous bobbin to ensure tightly woven stitches.

Counter   A small barrel with two dials that slips over the end of the needle. One dial counts the rows, and the other

BASIC AMERICAN NEEDLE LENGTHS USED IN THIS BOOK

straight needles: double-pointed, 7″ and 10″; single-pointed, 10″ and 14″
circular needles: 16″, 24″, 29″, 36″

KNITTING NEEDLE SIZES

United States	0	1	2	2	3	4	5	6	7	8	9	10
New United Kingdom	2	2¼	2¾	3	3¼	3½	3¾	4	4½	5	5½	6
Original United Kingdom	14	13	12	11	10	—	9	8	7	6	5	4
European (metric)	2	2½	2½	3	3½	3½	3½	4	4½	5	5½	6

KNITTING NEEDLE SIZES, *continued*

United States	10½	—	—	11	13	15	17	18	19	35	50
New United Kingdom	6½	7	7½	8	9	10	—	—	—	—	—
Original United Kingdom	3	2	1	0	00	000	—	—	—	—	—
European (metric)	6½	7	7½	8	9	10	12½	14	15½	19	25

CROCHET HOOK SIZES (MM)

A	B	C	D	E	F	G	H	I	J	K
1.5	2.0	2.5	3.0	3.5	4.0	4.5	5.0	5.5	6.0	7.0

counts the number of increases or decreases or any other bit of information needed for your stitchery. The main pitfall is that counters are not automatic; you must remember to turn the dials as you work.

Crochet Hook   A best friend to knitters, even those who don't crochet. This hooked needle is a permanent member of the rescue committee, especially for picking up dropped stitches, and is often used in seaming as well as trimming knitted garments.

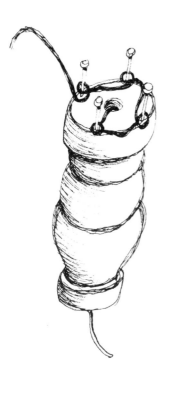

Holders   Large "safety pins" available in several sizes. They are used for holding a number of stitches from one portion of a garment while you work another portion.

Knitting Spool   A small cylinder with four nails at the top that often resembles a doll* (see directions for Rosebud Lariat). Thread the yarn through the top and out the bottom of the center hole, leaving the tail. Wrap the yarn two times around the outside of the nails. Pull the lower thread over the nail, creating a loop or stitch. Continue to wrap and loop, pulling work down through the center hole, thereby knitting in the round.

Markers   Usually round ivory or plastic circles of different diameters for various needle sizes that slip over the needle and move along while you work, to mark rows, seams, measuring points, increases/decreases, and so on.

Quilting Pins   Glass-headed extralong pins developed for quilters to penetrate several layers of fabric and batting. They are ideal for use in blocking knits, for they don't get lost in the fibers.

Ruler/Sizer   A needlework ruler is *not* the one you can't find around the house because someone never put it back in the desk drawer. It is a 6″ ruler with a notched edge that makes it easier to measure your gauge. It also comes with numbered holes that correspond to knitting needle and crochet hook sizes. Thus you can be sure, after losing the package the needles came in, that the needles are the correct size before you embark on your project.

Tape Measure   A very necessary ingredient to your success! A ruler or yardstick does not suffice because it is not flexible. Everyone thinks she knows her own measurements, but is surprised when she actually measures them—join the forces! It is not only important to measure yourself, but also to measure the garment as you go. Always measure on a flat surface—*carefully!*

Tapestry Needle   A needle with a blunt tip rather than a sharp one like that of a sewing or embroidery needle. Its purpose is twofold, at least in my mind. With a tapestry needle you are less likely to stab your fingertips, and you will not split the fibers as you sew, for it is more likely to slip between the stitches.

Tips Rubber or plastic caps that fit over the end of a double-pointed needle to keep the stitches from sliding off one end as you work the other. They are also handy when you want to park your work; they will prevent the stitches from dropping as you carry your project around.

BASIC TECHNIQUES

To make your design look fully professional and custom-made, here are the techniques used by experienced needle-crafters.

Bind Off

In most cases you will work the bind-off stitches in the same manner you have worked the project. However, for a tighter edge, don't work the stitches; *slip* the stitches while binding off. Conversely, for a looser edge, use a larger-sized needle and work the bind-off stitches as usual. (See also "Bind Off" in "Basic Stitchery.")

Ripping Out

We've all been on that bus. It's well worth it for results you will be proud and happy to wear. You must take care to use the same tender, loving care in unraveling as you did in working. Easier said than done! But don't let your frustration and fury destroy the fibers or possibly the design itself. Sometimes it helps to just leave the work alone for a while. After unraveling, wrap the yarn loosely into an open hank and tie it at either end. Dip it in tepid water, and allow it to air-dry. All the kinks will disappear. (See also "Rip Out" in "Before You Start" for the technique.)

Tie On

It's time for a new skein. Help! Don't fret, even in the middle of a row. Leave a 5″ tail of your working strand. Start your new skein with a 5″ tail, and finish your row. On the *wrong* side,

tie a *square knot* (important because it won't slip undone later). Be careful not to pull your work as you tie. Weave in the tails on the wrong side when you are finishing your project.

Weave In Tails

With a large-eyed tapestry needle, thread the ends of loose yarn tails. Work on the wrong side of the design and weave each tail into the stitchery. Do not pull tightly; it will cause puckering on the front side. Weave in one direction*, then weave in the opposite direction; cut excess yarn closely.

Blocking

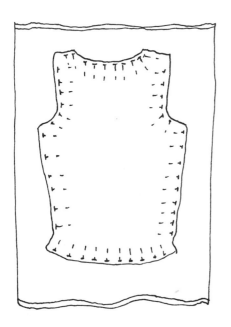

Blocking is easier than you think. Like so many other mysteries, it's a matter of know-how and proper tools. The basic requirements are nonrust pins, heavy terry-cloth towels, a tape measure, and patience. Dampen the garment in cool water and allow excess water to drip off. Roll *gently* in a towel to absorb more moisture. Unroll and lay flat on another dry towel. Pin waistline in place, measuring as you pin. Be sure the width and length of both sleeves are the same. Be sure the front and back are also the same width and length, as well as the armholes and shoulders. Use oodles of pins, one every inch or two; it's the pinning that *holds* the shape*.

Allow the garment to *dry naturally*. Heat, sun, steam, or hot irons are a disaster for the fibers. Anyone who hand-washes cashmeres knows how much more beautiful and softer they become with age—age and tender, loving care (but then, don't we all?).

Seams

There are several techniques for seaming, and most people develop one they prefer. However, it is often determined by the weight of the fiber and the type of design. Thus, it is wise to be aware of the choices. You can use a *single crochet stitch*: Pin the garment with right sides together, and work on the wrong side. Slip your crochet hook simultaneously through the edge stitch on each side that you wish to seam together and

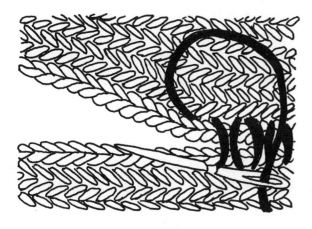

overcast stitch

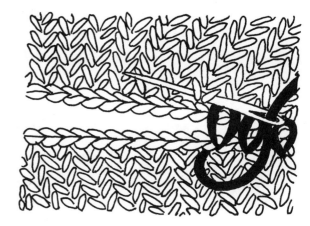

weaving (stockinette)

backstitch

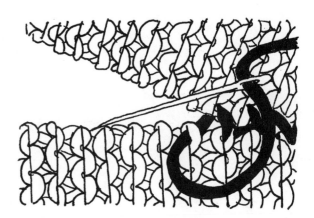

weaving (garter)

continue until the end of the seam. End with a slip stitch, and weave in the tail. This method takes a bit longer than others but gives a smooth, uniform seam. Some people prefer the quicker *overcast stitch**. Work a series of whipping stitches through the edge stitches along the seam line. You can also work in the basic *backstitch** used in hand-sewing a garment together; however, I do *not* recommend this, for it leaves a bulky seam and uneven front stitches. The most popular method is *weaving** from the right side of the garment, where you can see the results. Butt the edges together rather than overlap, which avoids bulk and does not sacrifice seamed stitches important to the proper fit*. Attach the yarn to one side, thread a tapestry needle, and slip the needle through the first loop on the opposite side, bringing it out through the second loop. Repeat on the other side. Then slip the needle into the *same* hole from which it emerged on the first side, and out the loop above it. Then back to the other side and repeat procedure to the end of the seam.

Circular Knits

When knitting in the round—with circular needles—there are a few helpful hints to observe. Some people simply refuse to work with circular needles because they don't want to fight back (take the kinks out of the needle). To unkink a needle, simply run the nylon core under hot water for a *few* minutes and relax. The kinks will smooth out. To avoid a gap when tying stitches together in casting on, slip a few stitches from one end of the needle to the other before tying them together.

Basic Stitchery

All the stitches required in the designs, as well as general information, follow. These instructions are written for right handers. Refer to the titles listed in the Bibliography for detailed left-handed instructions.

KNITTING

Cast On

Make a slip knot*(A), place it on the needle*(B) about 3″ from the end of the yarn, and tighten*(C). Holding this needle in your left hand and the other needle in your right hand, insert the tip of the second needle in the slip knot from left to right and front to back*(D). With your right hand, pass the yarn counter-clockwise around back and over tip of right-hand needle*(E). Then draw the yarn toward you through the knot and loop this stitch

Cast on

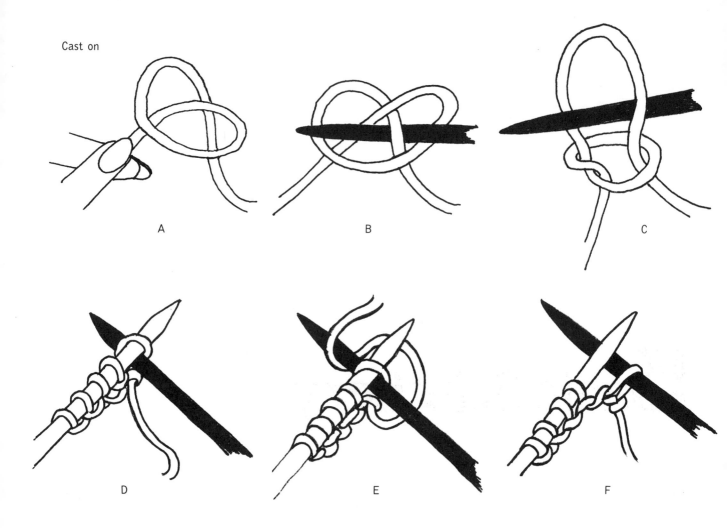

A

B

C

D

E

F

over the tip of the first needle, which holds the knot*(F). Repeat this procedure until you have cast on the desired number of stitches for your design and proper size. Once again, it is vitally important to *check your gauge,* for then you will know the correct number of stitches to cast on. The above method is called *knitting on* and is one of several methods. It is no better or more justified than other methods. It is simply a matter of personal preference. If you discover your cast-on stitches are too loose, cast on with a smaller needle.

Chevron Stitch

Cast on in multiples of 3 stitches. With the following pattern, your stitchery resembles a chevron or herringbone effect. Knit 2, make 1 stitch (pick up the horizontal loop lying between the needles and knit through the back of it), knit 4, slip 1 purlwise, knit 2 together, pass slipped stitch over, knit 4, then make 1. Repeat pattern—knit 2, make 1, knit 4, slip 1 purlwise, knit 2 together, pass over, knit 4, make 1—to end of row. Knit 2. Purl every alternate row.

Fan Stitch

To create the fan stitch, use a combination of wrap and knit stitches. The pattern consists of 11 rows. Row 1: Knit 2, wrap 1, slip 1, knit 1. Pass slip stitch over knit stitch. Knit 5, wrap 1, knit 2 together. Continue pattern across row. Purl row 2 and all alternate rows. Row 3: Knit 2, wrap 1, knit 1, slip 1, knit 1. Pass slip stitch over knit stitch. Knit 4, wrap 1, knit 2 together. Row 5: Knit 2, wrap 1, knit 2, slip 1, knit 1. Pass slip stitch over knit stitch. Knit 3, wrap 1, knit 2 together. Row 7: Knit 2, wrap 1, knit 3. Slip 1, knit 1. Pass slip stitch over knit stitch. Knit 2, wrap 1, knit 2 together. Row 9: Knit 2, wrap 1, knit 4. Slip 1, knit 1. Pass slip stitch over knit stitch. Knit 1, wrap 1, knit 2 together. Row 11: Knit 2, wrap 1, knit 5. Slip 1, knit 1. Pass slip stitch over knit stitch. Knit 1, wrap 1, knit 2 together.

Garter Stitch

A knitting-pattern stitch in which you work every row in knit stitches only. It gives a rippled or wavy look to the design, with a heavier texture than stockinette, and thus is sometimes used for ribbing or edges.

Lace Stitch

To create the lace stitch: Row 1; knit across. Row 2; knit 1, yarn over, knit 2 together; repeat across the row. These 2 rows define the lace stitch pattern.

Moss Stitch (or Seed Stitch)

The moss stitch is worked on an uneven number of stitches, working knit 1, purl 1 across the row, ending with a knit stitch for every row. Thus the knit and purl stitches alternate, creating a seed effect.

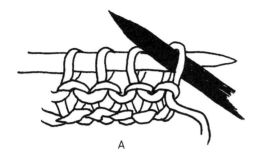

A

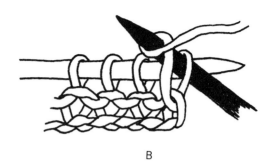

B

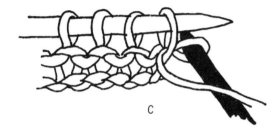

C

Purl

With stitches on the needle in your left hand and empty needle in your right hand, work the yarn from the front of the stitches. Slip the right-hand needle into the front of the first stitch, from right to left direction*(A). Wind the yarn counter-clockwise over and around the tip of this needle*(B); draw the yarn away from you toward the back and out through the back of the stitch*(C). Slip this stitch off the left-hand needle onto the right-hand needle, thus completing 1 purl stitch. Repeat this procedure across the row until all the stitches on the left-hand needle are transferred to the right-hand needle.

Reverse Stockinette

Achieved in the same manner as stockinette stitch. Knit 1 row, purl 1 row, but the purl row now becomes the outside of your design rather than the inside, as in stockinette.

Ribbing

Several stitches are used for ribbing; however, the most common is knit 1, purl 1 across the row, repeating this pattern on every row. This is worked on an even number of stitches. This type of rib stitch gives a great deal of elasticity to the garment and helps prevent stretching.

Slip Stitch

A stitch that you slip from the left- to the right-hand needle without working it.

Stockinette Stitch

A knitting-pattern stitch in which you work 1 row of knit stitches, and then 1 row of purl stitches, and continue to alternate knit and purl rows. It gives a smooth, even surface and is often found in machine knits.

Wave Stitch

The wave stitch is worked in multiples of 11 stitches. Row 1, knit; row 2, purl; row 3, purl 2 together twice, increase 1 stitch, knit into 1 stitch 3 times, increase 1 stitch, then purl 2 together twice. Repeat rhythm across the row. Row 4, purl. These 4 rows define the wave. Repeat 2 more times for ribbing.

Increase

To add stitches to those you are now working. To shape a garment to fit properly, it is essential to increase and decrease. To increase, work the stitch as usual* (A), but *do not* slip it off the left-hand needle* (B). Rather, work a second stitch in the back of the same stitch you have just worked* (C), and then slip both stitches to the right-hand needle. To increase when purling, work in the same manner (2 repeat stitches in the same

A

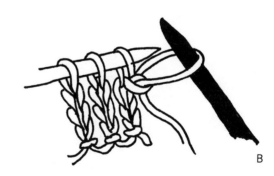

B

C

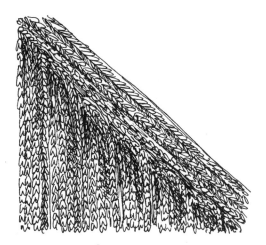

stitch), but insert needle into the front of the stitch. Another method is to work the yarn between the stitches as if it were a stitch in itself. *Full fashion* increase (or decrease) refers to the spacing of stitches to be increased (or decreased). The most common method is visible on set-in sleeves, when you have worked 2 or 3 stitches before (or after) the increase (or decrease), which lets these stitches show in a slight herringbone pattern along the edge of the seam*. The distinct advantage to this method is that you have an even edge when finished, rather than an occasional bulge or lump where the stitches have been increased (or decreased) at the beginning or end of a row. *Yarn over* is also used to increase stitches; however, this is usually in conjunction with a patterned stitch such as a lace stitch. On the knit side, bring the yarn to the front of the work, in between the stitches*(A), then bring the *yarn over* the right-hand needle, and around the tip at the back* (B), and knit the next stitch in the usual manner. On the purl side, wrap the yarn completely around the right-hand needle (from front to back) and purl the next stitch.

Yarn over

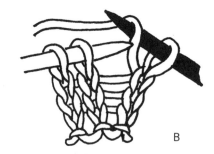

A

B

Decrease

To reduce stitches on your needle. On the knit side, slip the tip of the right-hand needle into the second stitch on the left-hand needle and then into the first stitch, working the 2 stitches together as if they were 1*(A). To decrease on the purl side, use the same procedure, with a purl stitch*(B). This method is used toward the beginning of a row or midway across the row. If you are decreasing at the end of the row, a different procedure is used in order to slant the stitches in the opposite direction. Slip 1 stitch without working it from the left- to the right-hand needle and knit the next stitch in the usual manner*(C); with the left-hand needle then pass the slipped stitch back over the knit

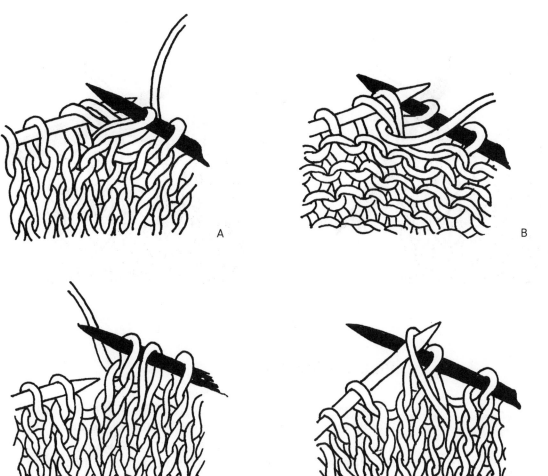

stitch*(D), off the tip of the needle, and let it drop in between the stitches (see also "Bind Off").

Bind Off

Repeat stitchery pattern as you bind off to shape a garment as well as end the last row of stitches. Work the first 2 stitches in the stitch pattern you have been using. Insert the tip of the left-hand needle (from left to right direction) into the first stitch worked*(A). Pass this first stitch over the second stitch worked (toward the left), off the tip of the right-hand needle, and let it drop in between the stitches*(B). Repeat, working 1 stitch, slipping 1 stitch off, until 1 stitch remains. Cut the yarn, leaving a 6″ tail, pull the end of the yarn through this last stitch, and tighten to prevent unraveling. If you use a larger needle than the one you have been using, it will prevent the bind-off edge from becoming too tight.

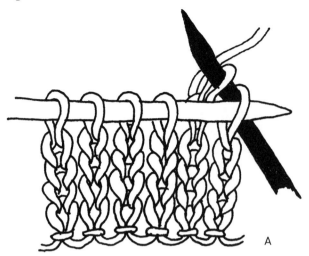

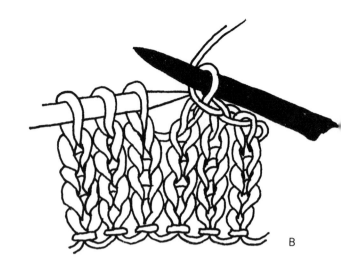

Pick Up Stitches

The direction in which you pick up the dropped stitches is *most* important. On the knit side, work from *front to back;* insert a crochet hook into the dropped stitch and pull the yarn of the row above it through this stitch, and slip it onto the needle*(A). If several rows of stitches have been dropped, repeat this procedure, working one stitch at a time until the last row, and then slip it onto the needle. On the purl side, insert crochet hook from *back to front* *(B).

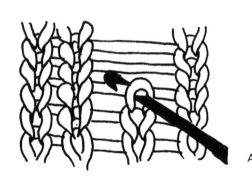

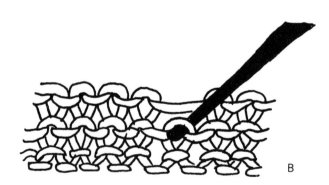

CROCHET

Crochet differs from knitting in many ways. The primary difference is that you are working with a single needle rather than two. This needle, or crochet hook, as it is called, is used to hook the yarn and pull it through previously worked stitches, thus developing patterns from a series of loops and chains. The versatility of the crochet hook and the variety of stitchery make crochet irresistible to many. If for no other reason than that of seaming or trimming knit designs, it is well worth learning the crochet basics. Needless to say, I dare you to stop there!

Foundation Chain

The foundation chain is the beginning of any crochet project, equivalent to the process of casting on in knitting, for it determines the number of stitches and thus the size of the design. Make a slip knot on the crochet hook, and hold the hook in your *right* hand, as you would a pencil. Wrap the working strand of yarn over the *left* ring finger, under the middle finger, and over the index finger, thus feeding the yarn at an even tension to the hook as you work. If you desire more tension, wrap the yarn around your little finger as well. To create chain stitches, hold the tail of the knot between your left thumb and index finger and, with your right hand, insert the hook under the yarn on your index finger, catching the yarn with the hook and drawing it through the previous loop*. Continue working chain stitches in this manner until the desired number of stitches are worked according to the pattern.

Single Crochet

Work the foundation chain to the desired length, then insert the crochet hook into the second loop from the hook end of the chain (skip the 1st loop) *(A), and draw the yarn through the loop and onto the hook, making 2 loops on the hook*(B); then draw the yarn through these 2 loops*(C), making 1 loop on the

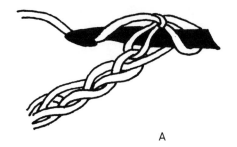

A

B

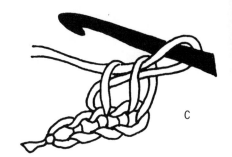

C

hook. This completes a single crochet stitch. Repeat this procedure in each of the chain stitches to complete a row. To turn and work back across in the opposite direction (row 2), make 1 additional chain stitch before turning in order to establish an even edge. Different effects are created by the manner in which you insert the hook into the previous stitches, i.e., under top of loop, under bottom of loop, or under both sides of loop. Experiment—it's fun.

Half Double Crochet

Work the foundation chain; wrap the yarn around the hook once, and insert the hook into the 3rd chain stitch from the end*(A); draw the yarn through the loop and onto the hook, making 3 loops on the hook*(B). Then draw the yarn through these 3 loops, thus completing a half double crochet stitch*(C). Continue to work in each chain stitch across the row, unless the pattern suggests otherwise. To turn and work the next row, work 2 additional chain stitches before starting the next row.

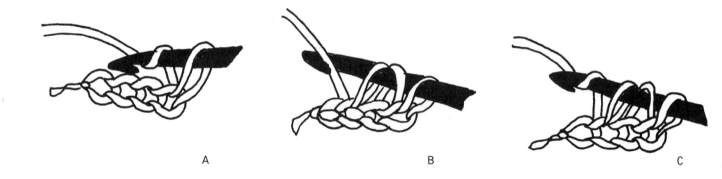

A   B   C

Double Crochet

Work the foundation chain; wrap the yarn once around the hook and insert hook into the 4th chain stitch from the hook. Draw the yarn through the loop and onto the crochet hook, making 3 loops on the hook*(A). Wrap the yarn around the hook once again and draw through only the first 2 loops on the hook, making 2 loops left on hook*; yarn over again, and

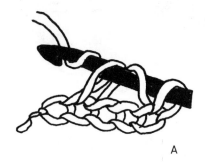

A

draw the yarn through these last 2 loops to complete one double crochet stitch*, leaving 1 loop on the hook. To turn, work 3 additional chain stitches before beginning the next row.

Triple Crochet

Wrap the yarn around the crochet hook twice; insert the hook into the fifth chain stitch from hook*(A). Wrap the yarn around the hook and draw through a loop, making 4 loops on the hook. Then wrap the yarn and draw through the first 2 loops only; do this again, leaving 2 loops on the hook. Wrap the yarn once again and draw through the last 2 loops, leaving 1 loop on the hook.

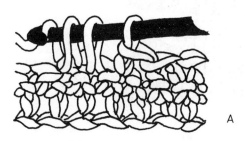

A

Turning

The way to progress from one row to the next. At the end of a single crochet row; work an extra single chain stitch* (for double crochet, work 2 chain stitches; for triple crochet, work 3 chain stitches). Then turn your design around in your hands, and continue to work across the row in the opposite direction.

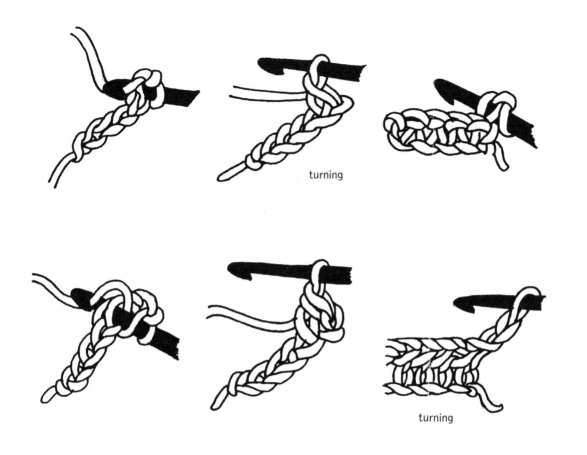

turning

turning

Increase

Work 2 stitches into the same loop. You also work 2 stitches into the same loop in order to work around a corner and prevent it from puckering.

Decrease

Draw a loop through 2 separate stitches, then yarn over and draw a loop through all 3 stitches on the crochet hook*.

decrease

Slip Stitch

The equivalent to a bind-off stitch in knitting. It is the manner in which you end the working strand of yarn, by drawing it through the loop of the last chain stitch in the row and simultaneously through the single stitch on the crochet hook in a single motion. It can also be used as a joining stitch or to bind and strengthen knit or crochet edges. If it is the final stitch of a project, cut the working strand, leaving a 7″ tail, and draw the end through the final 2 loops left on the crochet hook.

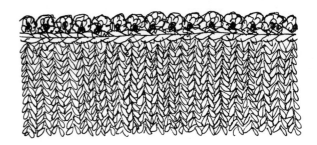

Picot Stitch

The number of chain stitches (spaces) worked between the picot stitches defines the pattern; these chain stitches may vary from 1 to 5. The fewer stitches used, the lacier the effect. To start picot stitch, work a single crochet stitch in each of the first 3 stitches (or any other desired spacing); chain 3, make 1 slip stitch in last worked stitch of previous row. Repeat space pattern, chain 3. Repeat picot stitch. One may chain 4 or 5 stitches to form picot, depending on desired length. Most often used to trim the edges of finished designs*.

Shell Stitch

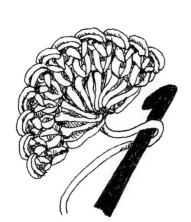

This stitch resembles a scallop shell as you work 5 triple crochet stitches in the same space. Work the foundation chain to desired length. The rhythm is as follows: To turn, chain 3; work 5 triple crochet in 4th chain from hook (shell stitch); skip 3 stitches, work 1 slip stitch in next stitch (holds the other side of the shell stitch in place); skip next 3 stitches, work 5 triple crochet in next stitch; repeat this rhythm across the row. Each new row fits into the space left between the shell stitches in the previous row. To turn, work 3 chain stitches, then work 1 slip stitch in the top center of the first shell stitch, and 5 triple crochet stitches in the space between the first and second shell stitch of the previous row; repeat procedure back and forth across each row.

Bind Off:

See "Crochet: Slip Stitch" (p. 38).

EMBROIDERY

There are many embroidery stitches that can embellish knitwear designs. The few stitches used in this book are merely a tease, suggested with the hope that you will venture further. With the exception of the bullion stitch, all of them can be easily mastered by a novice.

The Bullion Stitch

This stitch can be a bit tricky to master, and I suggest you practice a few stitches on some scrap fabric before applying them directly on your design. This is *not* a difficult stitch, merely different—and it takes most people a few tries to get the feel of it. You can use bullion roses in lieu of buttons, with a single crochet chain looped as a closure. Keep trying this stitch. It is truly exquisite—especially when worked in ombré yarn, with the pale tone in the center of a flower. The mechanics are the same as for the French knot. Wrap your needle several times (rather than once or twice) before inserting it back through the fabric*(A). Hold the wraps firmly as you slowly slide the needle through, keeping the yarn close to the surface*(B). In making flowers, allow the longer stitches to curl around one another*(C). Make each stitch longer than the previous one, starting at the center with 7 wraps, then 9, 12, 18, 21, and 25. Bullion stitches also make excellent leaves and can be held in place with a single small tie-down stitch (as in the lazy daisy) or allowed to fall free. Practice—it is well worth it.

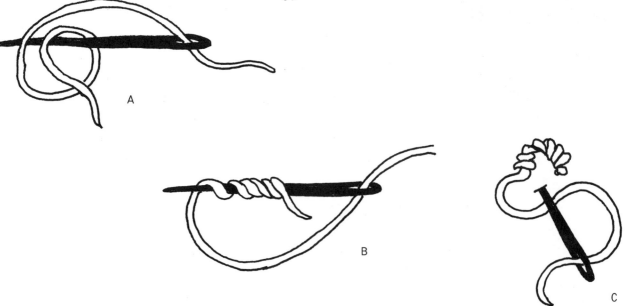

A

B

C

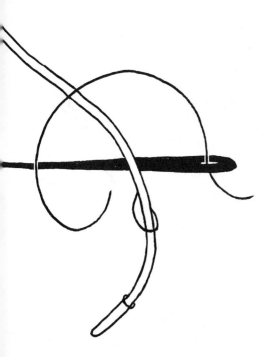

Couching

The technique in which a heavy fiber is sewn to the surface, using a very fine fiber*. If you want the small stitches to be "invisible," use a thread that matches the thicker fiber. However, some fascinating effects are created by purposely using an extreme-contrast color fiber to tack down. This is often apparent in the exquisite metallic embroidery where bright purples and reds and greens are used to tack down gold and silver metallic fibers.

Duplicate Stitch

So called because it duplicates, or traces the outline of, the stockinette stitch. Duplicate stitch is considered an embroidery chain stitch. Using your tapestry needle, bring yarn from back to front through the base of a stockinette stitch*(A). Working from left to right, place needle under the entire stockinette stitch above it; draw yarn through*(B). Re-insert needle at the base of first stockinette stitch and bring out again at base of next stitch in your embroidery pattern. Make your stitches the same gauge as that of your knitwear. This stitch enables you to create intricate patterns after you have finished your knit design, rather than working with several bobbins and graphs as you knit. If using a graph, keep in mind that knit stitches are wider than they are tall. Therefore, the design will look wider than it does on your graph.

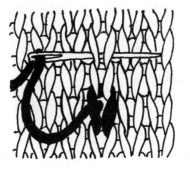

A

B

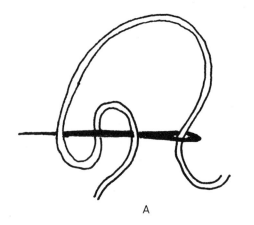

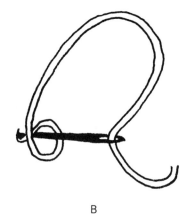

A	B	C

French Knot

Wrap the yarn once or twice around the needle*(A) close to the fabric and replace the needle near the point at which it originated*(B). The size of the knot varies with the thickness of thread, the size of the needle, and the number of times you wrap the yarn. French knots are most versatile and can be worked en masse or scattered, as mini-flowers*(C) or an entire flock of sheep. In working flowers, French knots in an ombré yarn are quite effective for subtle shading.

Lazy Daisy

Considered a detached chain stitch made in 2 steps. First work a simple chain stitch by looping the thread under the needle as you draw it through*(A). Holding it in place, then work a small tie-down stitch at the top of the loop*(B). When several stitches are worked in a circle, they make marvelous flowers, especially with a series of French knots grouped together in the center. For leaves, try working 1 stitch a bit smaller inside the first stitch, and end with a single straight stitch down the center as a vein.

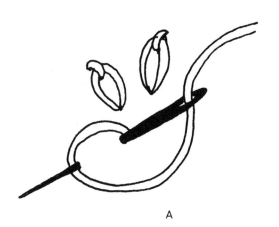

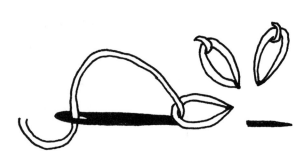

A	B

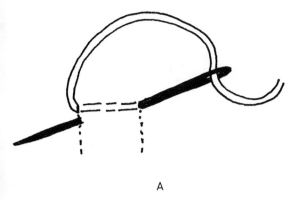

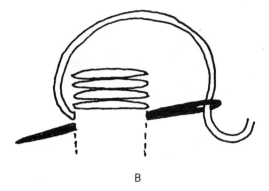

A   B

Satin Stitch

A series of straight stitches that are usually worked in the same direction*(A) to form a smooth, well-defined area*(B). They can be flat, couched, or padded. A padded satin stitch gives a raised, three-dimensional effect to the surface, and you can create the look of trapunto by merely working the satin stitch first in one direction, then repeating a second layer in the opposite direction. A simple but effective stitch.

Threaded Running Stitch

Work a uniform series of running stitches; then, with a blunt needle, weave yarn through these running stitches. Different patterns develop according to the direction in which you weave the secondary yarn. When woven in the same direction, it creates a twisted, vinelike effect*(A); when woven in alternate directions, a wavy, scalloplike effect results*(B). It is also very decorative when a contrast-color yarn is used, or one of the same color but of a different tone. You can also weave 2 rows, each in an opposite direction, and create a row of ovals. It's not only versatile, it's fun.

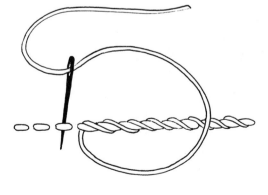

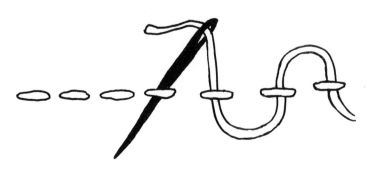

A   B

Designs

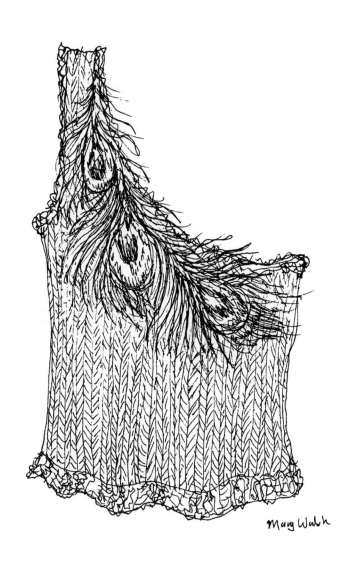

TOGA

BEGINNER LEVEL

DETAILS

Stitch	rib: knit wave stitch
	bodice: knit in the round and stockinette
	trim: single crochet
Gauge	5 stitches, 6 rows/inch (ribbon)
Notes	Peacock feathers may be replaced by other trim, or the toga may be left untrimmed.

MATERIALS

1 skein	Melrose Pearlite: #140, black
4 rolls	Gemini Charmeuse ribbon: #311, malachite
3	large peacock feathers (optional)
	#5 circular knitting needle, 24″ long
	#7 circular knitting needle, 24″ long
	#7 straight knitting needles, 10″ long
	#5 crochet hook (size E)

DIRECTIONS

With #5 needle and 2 strands of Pearlite yarn, cast on 150 (158, 166) stitches. Work in wave stitch (see "Basic Stitchery: Wave

Stitch"). Center pattern on number of stitches on your needle, worked in multiples of 11 stitches. Change to #7 circular needle and single strand of ribbon. Row 1, knit in round; row 2, knit 4, knit 2 together around entire row, then knit for 11 (12, 13) inches or desired length to armhole. Separate half of the stitches for back and place on holder; continue blouse in stockinette stitch on #7 straight needles. **Front:** Work neckline edge and armhole edge simultaneously. For armhole edge only, bind off 4 stitches at beginning of next row. Decrease 1 stitch every other row, 4 (5, 5) times. Continue remainder of armhole edge evenly. At neckline edge, bind off 13 (18, 23) stitches. Decrease 1 stitch every other row, until 6 stitches remain at shoulder; bind off. **Back:** Work in same manner as front, but in reverse. **Finish:** Sew together at shoulder; weave in tails. With crochet hook and a single strand of Pearlite, work 2 rows of single crochet around armhole and neckline. Sew on feathers or other decorative trim.

LONG-SLEEVED BLOUSE

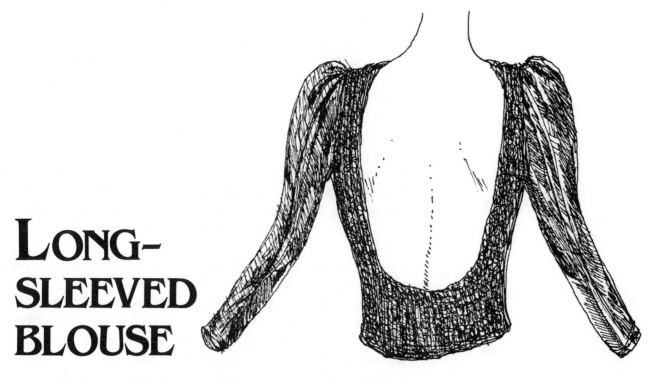

May Welch

BEGINNER LEVEL

DETAILS

Stitch	bodice: stockinette trim: single crochet
Gauge	4 stitches, 3 rows/inch
Notes	Fabric sleeves are sewn onto bodice; the blouse may also be left sleeve- less.

MATERIALS

5 skeins	Scandinavian Imports/Hovland chenille #4041, black
1 yard	fabric of your choice #7 knitting needles, 14″ long #10 crochet hook (size J) blouse pattern in your size with gathered sleeve design

DIRECTIONS

Back: With #7 needles and single strand of chenille yarn, cast on 46 (54, 62) stitches. Work in stockinette for 6 (6, 7) inches.

Bind off 16 (20, 20) stitches at center back. Tie on another ball of yarn at other side. Decrease 1 stitch at neck edge every row, 5 times. Work each side evenly until 12 (12, 12½) inches to armhole. Bind off 2 stitches at beginning of armhole edges. Decrease 1 stitch every other row, 2 times. Continue evenly for 6 (6½, 7) inches. Increase 1 stitch at neckline edge every other row, 3 times; work evenly to shoulder until 19 (20, 21) inches long. **Front:** Cast on 46 (54, 62) stitches. Work evenly 12 (12, 12½) inches to armhole. Bind off 2 stitches at beginning of next 2 rows. Decrease 1 stitch either end of knit row, 2 times. Work evenly 16½ (17, 17½) inches to neckline. Bind off 8 (10, 10) stitches at center front. Tie on yarn. Decrease 1 stitch at neck edge every row, 4 times. Work evenly until 18½ (19½, 20½) inches long. Increase 1 stitch at neck edge every other row, 2 times. Work evenly until 19 (20, 21) inches long; bind off at shoulder.

Finish: Butt edges at shoulders and sides; whip-stitch seams together with thread. With crochet hook and a single strand of chenille, work 1 row single crochet from inside around hemline. Work 2 rows single crochet around neckline, 1st row from inside and 2nd row from outside. If you want to wear it sleeveless, crochet 3 rows of single crochet around armhole. Choose a dress or blouse pattern with a gathered sleeve design in your size. Pin, cut, and sew sleeves according to pattern instructions. Sew sleeves into knit bodice, using ¼" seam; zigzag around inside edges of armhole, or use bias binding to avoid fraying.

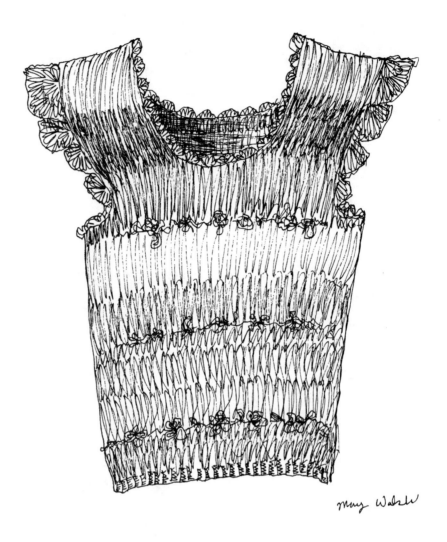

FLORAL STRIPES

INTERMEDIATE LEVEL

DETAILS

Stitch	rib: knit 1, purl 1
	bodice: knit stitch (in the round); stockinette
	trim: crochet shell stitch
	embroidery: threaded running, lazy daisy, French knot, bullion
Gauge	8 stitches, 8 rows/inch
Notes	What to do with leftovers? Use yardage (see "Fibers") as a guide to substitute your own leftovers or work your own stripes at random.

MATERIALS

Leftovers and innovation make up the majority of the materials for this blouse, hence quantity is only an estimate.

10 skeins	#3 DMC perle cotton #504, pale green
7 skeins	#3 DMC perle cotton #503, medium green
5 skeins	#3 DMC perle cotton #501, dark green
1 skein	#3 DMC perle cotton #745, yellow
1 skein	#3 DMC perle cotton #543, light rose
1 skein	#3 DMC perle cotton #3064, deep rose

3 skeins	Yarn Lofts ribbon #71, chartreuse
2 skeins	Yarn Lofts ribbon #14 yellow
2 skeins	Yarn Lofts ribbon #76 rose
3 skeins	Yarn Lofts ribbon #58, gray
2 skeins	Yarn Lofts ribbon #75, dark green
2 skeins	Yarn Lofts ribbon #73, sage
	#2 circular knitting needle, 24″ long
	#5 circular knitting needle, 24″ long
	#5 crochet hook (size E)
	large stitch holder

DIRECTIONS

With #2 needle and a single strand of pale green perle cotton, cast on 176 (184, 192) stitches. Tie ends together. Work rib stitch—knit 1, purl 1—for ¾ inch. Break off yarn and tie in medium green; repeat rib; then break yarn and tie in dark green and repeat. Break yarn. Change to #5 needle and tie in chartreuse ribbon; knit stockinette for 2½ (2¾, 3) inches. Knit yellow ribbon for 2 inches. Knit rose ribbon for 2 inches. Knit gray ribbon for 2½ (3, 3½) inches. Knit dark green ribbon for 1 inch to armhole. Place half of the stitches on holder for back. Knit remainder of blouse in stockinette stitch. **Front:** Armhole: Cast off 4 stitches at beginning of next 2 rows, then decrease 1 stitch either end of knit row 3 times. On last row of green ribbon, bind off 14 stitches at center front. Tie on dark green perle cotton at either side of neckline. Simultaneously decrease 1 stitch every other row at armhole edges 4 more times; decrease neckline edge 1 stitch every other row 10 times. Continue until there are 3 inches of dark green. Work medium green perle for 2½ inches. Work light green perle for 1½ (2, 2½) inches; bind off. **Back:** With dark green ribbon, decrease 1 stitch every other row 3 times at armhole edges. Work medium green perle for 3 inches, decrease at armhole 4 more times. Work sage ribbon 1 inch; bind off 18 stitches at center back; tie on yarn; decrease 1 stitch every other row 6 times at neckline edge. Continue armhole edge straight. Work light green perle for 2½ (3, 3½) inches; bind off. **Finish:** Sew at shoulders. With crochet hook and light green perle, work a single row of shell stitch around neckline and first row around armholes; start 2nd row in center of first shell stitch. Start 3rd row in center of 4th shell stitch; bind off. *Embroidery* (see "Basic Stitchery"): for *vines,* use threaded running stitch in medium green perle; for *leaves,* use lazy daisy stitch in both medium and light green perle; for *yellow flowers* (5 petals each), use 2 lazy daisy and 1 straight stitch, yellow perle, use a single rose perle French knot at the center; for *light green perle flowers,* use 6 clustered French knots with scattered chartreuse perle knots along the vine; for *rose perle flowers,* use clustered small and medium bullion stitches in light rose and deep rose perle.

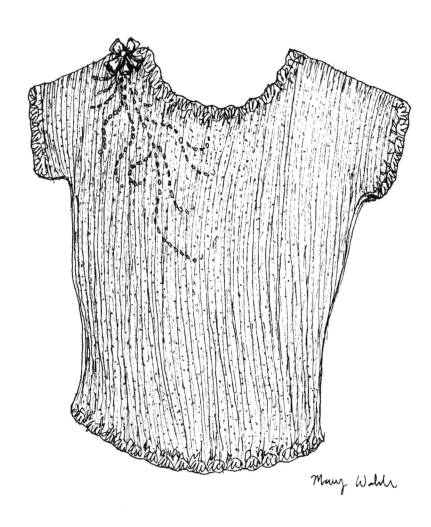

GOLD BEAD BLOUSE

INTERMEDIATE LEVEL

DETAILS

Stitch	rib: chevron knit
	bodice: stockinette
	trim: crochet shell stitch; single crochet
Gauge	6 stitches, 8 rows/inch
Note	Presewn beaded appliqué may be used.

MATERIALS

1 skein	Unger Ariane #16, copper
8 skeins	Unger Ariane #18, gold
1 string	copper/glass beads
1	beading needle
1	decorative button, pin, or appliqué
	#5 knitting needles, 14″ long
	#5 crochet hook (size E)
	beading thread

DIRECTIONS

Back: With #5 needles, 1 strand of copper, and 1 strand of gold yarn, cast on 95 (106, 115) stitches. Work evenly in chevron

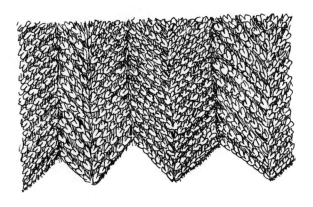

stitch for 8 rows*. (See "Knitting: Chevron Stitch.") Change to 2 strands of gold yarn; work 4 rows in chevron stitch. Change to stockinette stitch and work evenly 10½ (11½, 12½) inches, to armhole. Add 4 stitches at beginning of next 2 rows. Increase 1 stitch either end of knit row, 2 (3, 3) times; continue sleeve edge straight. Neckline: start 1 inch above armhole; bind off 30 stitches at center back. Tie on additional yarn to other side. Decrease 1 stitch at neck edge every row, 6 (8, 10) times, and then every other row, 3 (4, 5) times. Continue armhole evenly until it measures 7 (7½, 8) inches. Bind off at shoulder. **Front:** Repeat back to armhole. Start neckline 3½ inches above armhole; work in same manner as back until it measures the same length.

Finish: Sew together at shoulders and side seams; weave in tails. With crochet hook, 1 strand of gold, and 1 strand of copper, work 2 rows of shell stitch around neckline and sleeves. Then, with a single strand of copper yarn, work 2 rows of single crochet around hem, sleeves, and neckline. Use a beading needle and thread to restring and sew on beads*. Old shoe buckles, buttons, or unique fasteners also add finesse.

Bavarian Blouse

ADVANCED LEVEL

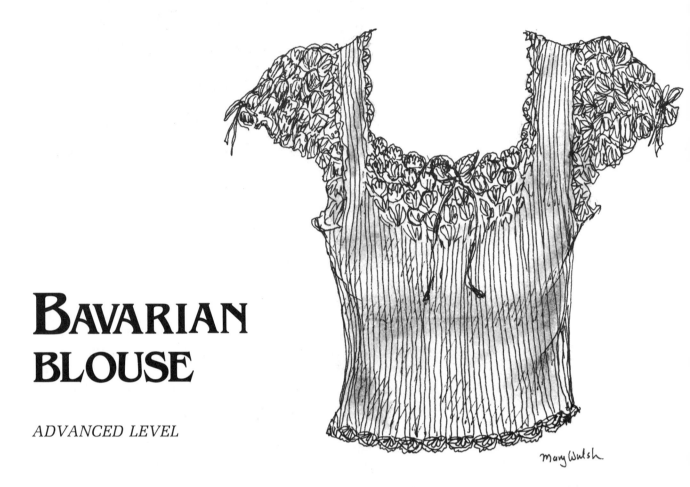

DETAILS

Stitch	bodice: stockinette
	trim: crochet shell stitch
Gauge	stockinette: 5 stitches, 5 rows/inch
Note	Weave narrow ribbon through edges of bodice and sleeves for puffed shape.

MATERIALS

5 skeins	mohair blend, mint
3½ yards	narrow ribbon
	#5 knitting needles, 14″ long
	#5 crochet hook (size E)

DIRECTIONS

Front: With #5 needles and single strand of mohair-blend yarn, cast on 70 (77, 84) stitches. Work evenly in stockinette stitch for

Butterfly Bandeau

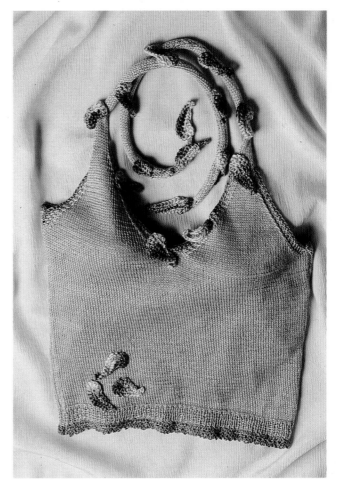

Leaf Halter

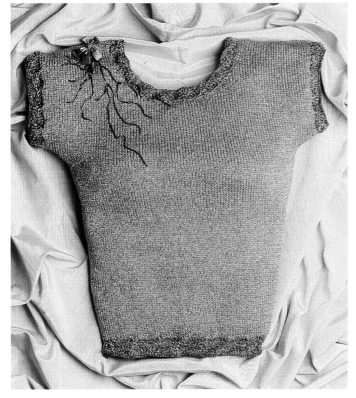

Gold Bead Blouse

Ribbon Clutch

Pheasant Camisole

Long-Sleeved Jacket

Sable-Tail Lariat

Silk Ombré

Short-Sleeved
Jacket

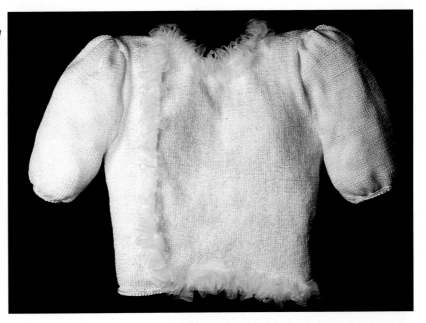

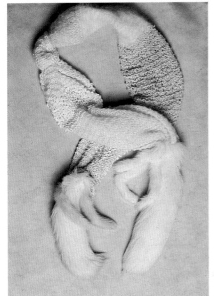

Ivory
Shawl

Tasseled
Purse

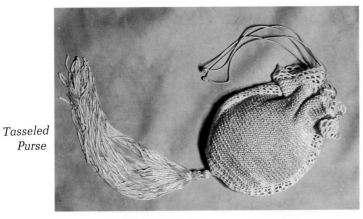

Feather Bandeau

Puff-Sleeved Blouse

Shell
Necklace

Rose Bandeau

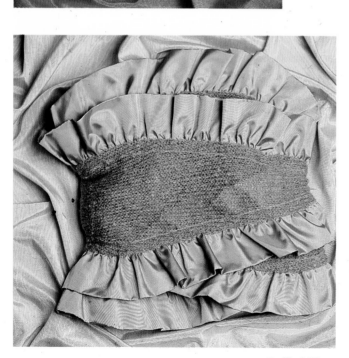

Rosebud
Lariat

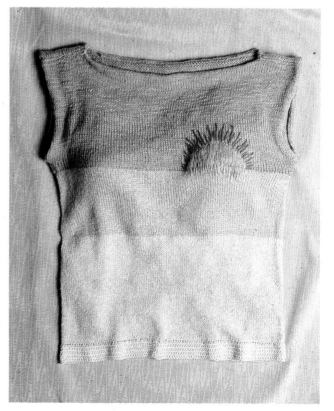

Ruffled Wrap

Sunrise Scoop

Floral Belt

Floral Stripes

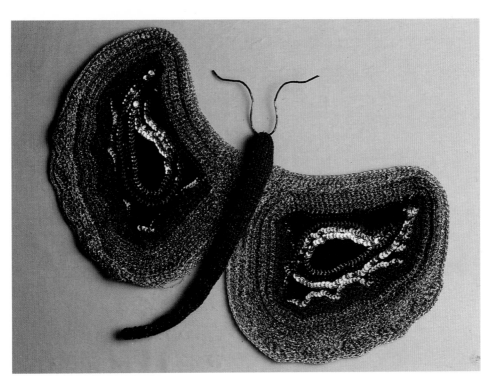

Butterfly Wrap

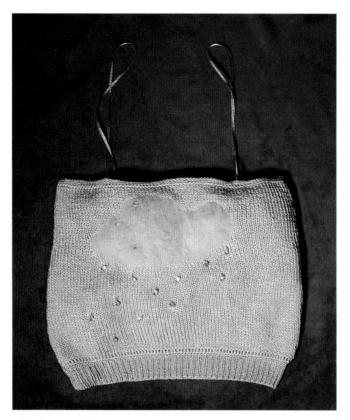

Cloud Camisole

Mixed Media Scoop

Vertical Stripes

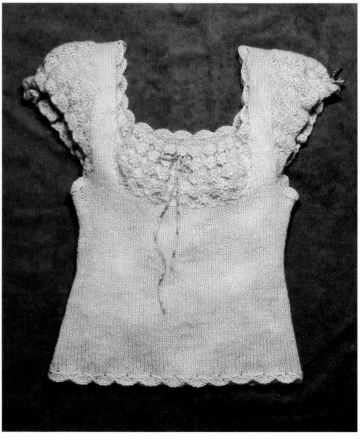

Bavarian Blouse

Lava Halter

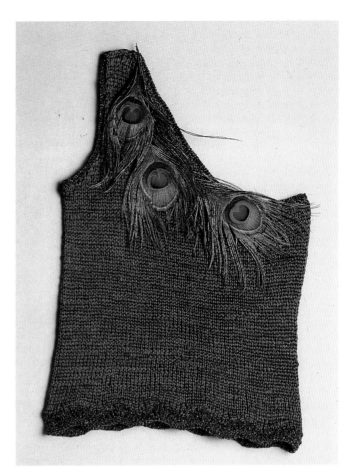

Toga

Black Shawl

Long-Sleeved Blouse

Stained-Glass Camisole

6 rows. Decrease 1 stitch either end of row, repeat every 7th row, 4 times. Continue working evenly for 1 inch. Increase 1 stitch either end of row, every 5th row, 3 times to armhole. Bind off 4 stitches at armhole edges beginning of next 2 rows; decrease 1 stitch either end of knit row 3 more times to neckline. Bind off 15 stitches at center front; tie on another ball of yarn; work remainder of the stitches. Decrease 1 stitch at neck edge every knit row, 3 times. Keep sleeve edge even, and continue 10 (10½, 12) inches from neckline; bind off at the shoulder.

Back: Repeat front and front armhole; start back neckline 14 (14½, 15) inches above hemline, shaping neckline same as front. Bind off at shoulder seam when it equals front length.

Finish: Weave in tails; sew front to back at shoulders and sides. With crochet hook and single strand of yarn, work 1 row shell stitch along hemline. **Sleeves** (14 rows): With crochet hook, work first row of shell stitch around armhole; start second row 3 shell stitches from underarm (side seam). Work 12 more rows, each row 1 shell stitch shorter than previous row.

Bodice (8 rows): With crochet hook and shell stitch, work 1st row around neckline; continue back and forth across front for 7 more rows. Weave ribbon through last row of sleeves and neckline, beginning at the center; draw ribbon together, and tie in a small bow.

PUFF-SLEEVED BLOUSE

ADVANCED LEVEL

DETAILS

Stitch	sleeves: stockinette
	bodice: reverse stockinette
	trim: moss stitch; single crochet
Gauge	4 stitches, 5 rows/inch
Notes	Feather rows are alternately knit with mohair. Blouse may be knit in mohair and feathers, or another embellishment may be sewn on later. Made sleeveless, this is great as a vest.

MATERIALS

11 balls	Anny Blatt mohair et soie, white
3 bags	Anny Blatt feathers, white
	#5 knitting needles, 10″ long
	#8 knitting needles, 10″ long
	#5 crochet hook (size E)

DIRECTIONS

Front: With #8 needle and 2 strands of mohair, cast on 50 (56, 62) stitches. Work evenly in reverse stockinette for 11 (11½, 12) inches. **Neckline and armhole:** Work neckline edge and armhole edge simultaneously. For neckline, work across one half of stitches to center front; bind off 1 stitch. Tie on yarn. Decrease 1 stitch at neck edge every other row until 8 stitches remain; continue evenly. Start armhole 6 rows after you start neckline. Bind off 3 stitches at armhole edge; decrease 1 stitch every other row, 2 times. Continue until piece measures 19 (20, 21) inches long. Bind off at shoulder. **Back:** Repeat front. **Sleeves:** With #5 needle and single strand of mohair, cast on 39 (43, 47) stitches. Work in moss stitch (See "Basic Stitchery: Moss Stitch") for 8 rows. Change to #8 needle and work in reverse stockinette, increasing on 1st knit row to 80 (88, 96) stitches; purl next row. Work 2 more rows of stockinette. Tie on feather yarn. Work 2 rows feathers, 2 rows mohair, 2 rows feathers, 4 rows mohair, thus establishing pattern. Repeat pattern. Manipulate feathers to front (purl) side as you work for 3½ (4, 4½) inches. To shape armhole, bind off 3 stitches at beginning of next 2 rows. Decrease 1 stitch either end of every other row, 7 times. Work evenly until 5 (5¼, 5½) inches from armhole. Bind off 3 stitches at beginning of next 4 rows. Work 2 stitches together all across the row for 2 rows (to gather and puff sleeve). Bind off remaining stitches.

Finish: Block bodice and weave tails. Crochet sleeves to bodice; this supports weight of feathered sleeves. Weave side seams and sleeve seams together. With crochet hook and single strand of mohair, work 1 row of single crochet around neckline from inside. Work 3 rows of single crochet around hemline.

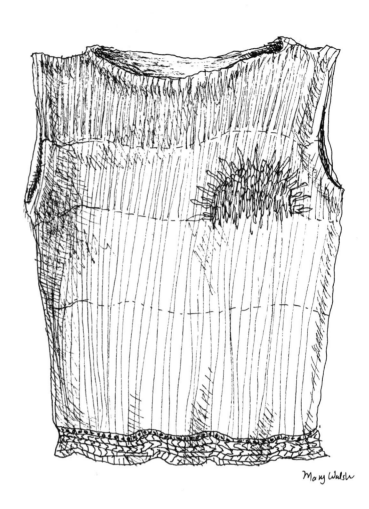

SUNRISE SCOOP

BEGINNER LEVEL

DETAILS

Stitch	rib: half double crochet bodice: knit in the round and stockinette
Gauge	6½ stitches, 8 rows/inch
Note	Embroidery may be worked in floss or perle cotton, rather than silk.

MATERIALS

2 skeins	Welcomme/La Soie #02, pale pink
1 skein	Welcomme/La Soie #11, apricot
1 skein	Tahki/Shan dusty rose
1 skein	Tahki/Shan lavender
3 skeins	#3 DMC perle cotton #712, cream
1 skein each	silk or perle pink, rose, umber
	#5 circular knitting needle, 24″ long
	#5 knitting needles, 14″ long
	#5 crochet hook (size E)

DIRECTIONS

With #5 circular needle and a single strand of pale pink yarn, cast on 190 (196, 202) stitches. Work knit stitch in the round for 6½ (7, 7½) inches. Break off yarn. Tie on apricot yarn at side seam; knit for 3½ (4, 4½) inches. Leave front half of stitches on round needle. **Back:** Tie on dusty rose yarn. Work on #5 straight needles in stockinette stitch. Increase 1 stitch either end of every knit row, 3 times. Armhole: Add 4 stitches at either end. Continue evenly until 5 inches from armhole. Break off yarn. Tie on lavender; work 3 inches to neckline. Neckline: Bind off 10 stitches beginning of next 6 rows; bind off remaining stitches at shoulder. **Front:** Repeat procedure on #5 straight needles.

Finish: Hemline: With crochet hook and cream perle cotton, work 1 row single crochet from front side. Work 3 rows half double crochet; turn and work 1 more row half double crochet from inside. Weave in all tails. *Embroidery*: With pink yarn, work a satin stitch in half-moon shape. Add several straight stitches with umber yarn at the bottom, intersecting pink yarn. Work sun's rays with rose yarn in long stitches*. Roll neckline and armhole edges to inside and hem in place*.

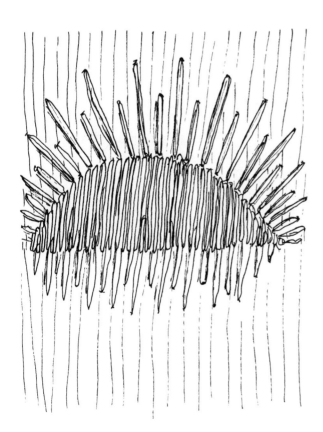

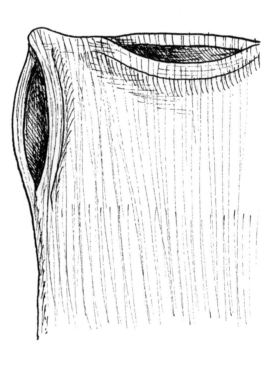

MIXED MEDIA SCOOP

INTERMEDIATE LEVEL

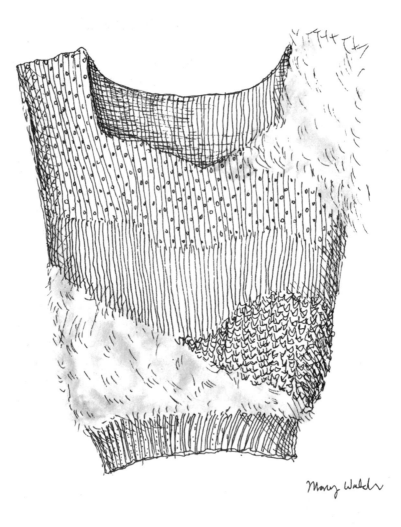

Mary Walsh

DETAILS

Stitch	rib: knit 1, purl 1
	bodice: stockinette
	trim: single crochet
Gauge	7 stitches, 8 rows/inch
Notes	A mixture of yarns gives you an inter-play of texture and color. Use yarns of similar weight for a uniform gauge.

MATERIALS

4 skeins	Melrose Rayonette baby gray
3 skeins	Melrose Belangor #807, gray (angora)
3 skeins	Yarn Lofts ribbon #73, sage green
1 skein	Tahki Daphne #953, aqua
4 skeins	DMC floss #927, sage
1 string	beads, pearl gray (optional)
1	beading needle
	#1 knitting needles, 14″ long
	#5 knitting needles, 14″ long
	#5 crochet hook (size E)
	sewing thread
	stitch holder

DIRECTIONS

Back: With #1 needles and Rayonette, cast on 184 (196, 206) stitches. Work in rib pattern—knit 1, purl 1—for 2 (2½, 2½) inches. Change to #5 needles and stockinette stitch; work evenly 11½ (12, 12½) inches to armhole. Cast on 4 stitches at beginning of next 2 rows; work armhole evenly. Start neckline 5 inches above armhole; bind off 18 stitches at center back. Tie on yarn. Bind off 5 stitches every other row at neckline edge 4 times; bind off at shoulders. **Front:** (see Basic Equipment: Bobbins) Repeat rib, then follow graph* for each design area—section 1, angora; section 2, ribbon; section 3, Daphne; section 4, floss; section 5, repeat angora. Repeat armhole as for back. Neckline: Start 1 inch above armhole, at center front. Separate sides. Place one side on stitch holder. Decrease neckline 1 stitch every other row, 8 times. Decrease every row 16 (18, 20) times. Stockinette to shoulder; bind off when front measures same length as back.

Finish: Sew side and shoulder seams. With crochet hook and Rayonette, work 1 row of single crochet around neckline. Optional: With sewing thread and a beading needle, sew beads on section 4 (floss), skipping 1 stitch in between each bead. Alternate placement of beads by 1 stitch to create a symmetrical pattern.

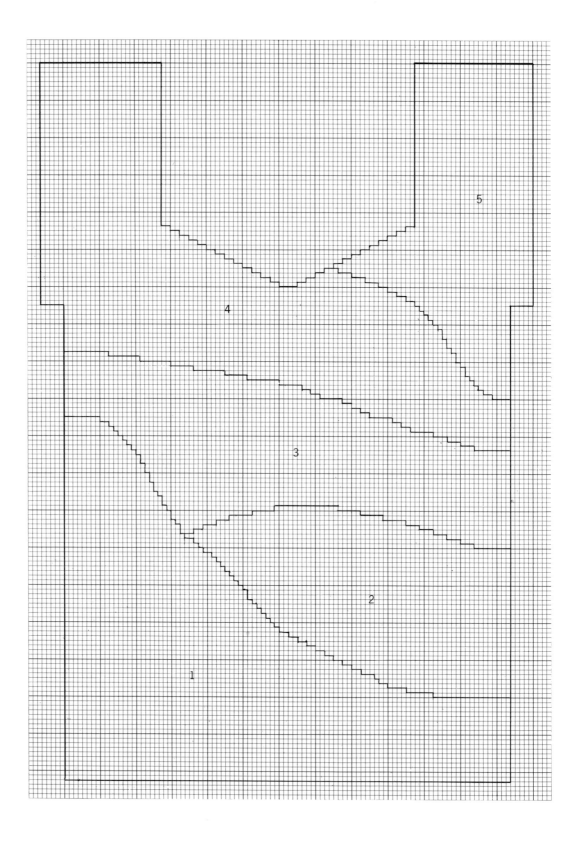

VERTICAL STRIPES

INTERMEDIATE LEVEL

DETAILS

Stitch	bodice: garter; stockinette trim: single crochet
Gauge	#5: 7 stitches, 9 rows/inch #7: 5 stitches, 8 rows/inch
Notes	The entire garment is worked side-ways, which avoids bobbins. If you weave tails carefully and crochet the seams, the sweater is reversible.

MATERIALS

2 skeins	Sheepish Grin ombré bouclé
1 skein	Melrose Rayonette, grape
1 skein	Melrose Rayonette, mulberry
2 skeins	Melrose Rayonette, lilac
	#5 knitting needles, 14″ long (for Rayonette)
	#7 knitting needles, 14″ long (for bouclé)
	#5 crochet hook (size E)
	elastic thread, available in complementary colors

DIRECTIONS

Front: Starting at sleeve edge, with #5 needles and mulberry yarn, cast on 50 stitches; work stockinette for 10 rows, then follow this chart:

needle #	yarn	stitch	rows
7	bouclé	stockinette	8

Add 64 (70, 76) stitches to underarm with:

5	lilac	stockinette	6
7	bouclé	stockinette	4
5	mulberry	garter	4
7	bouclé	stockinette	8
5	mulberry	garter	4
5	lilac	stockinette	6

On the sixth row, bind off 14 (20, 26) stitches from shoulder edge for neckline; continue to decrease 1 stitch at neck edge every other row, 4 times.

7	bouclé	stockinette	6
5	lilac	stockinette	2
5	grape	stockinette	4
7	bouclé	stockinette	6
5	mulberry	garter	4
7	bouclé	stockinette	4

Center front:

5	lilac	garter	6
5	grape	stockinette	4
7	bouclé	stockinette	4
5	mulberry	garter	4
7	bouclé	stockinette	4
5	mulberry	stockinette	2
5	grape	stockinette	4

Increase neck 1 stitch every other row, 4 times.

5	lilac	stockinette	6

Add 14 (20, 26) stitches for sleeve.

7	bouclé	stockinette	6
5	mulberry	garter	4
7	bouclé	stockinette	4
5	lilac	garter	6
7	bouclé	stockinette	7

On 7th row, bind off 70 stitches from waist, leaving sleeve stitches.

| 5 | grape | stockinette | 6 |

Decrease 1 stitch every other row, 4 times.

| 7 | bouclé | stockinette | 8 |
| 5 | mulberry | stockinette | 10 |

Bind off on 11th row. **Back:** Repeat procedure.

Finish: Weave in tails securely. Sew or crochet shoulder and side seams. With crochet hook and lilac yarn, work 1 row of single crochet from inside and 2 rows from outside around neckline and sleeves. Rayon yarn has a tendency to stretch; thus a fine elastic thread should be combined with it for the crochet edge.

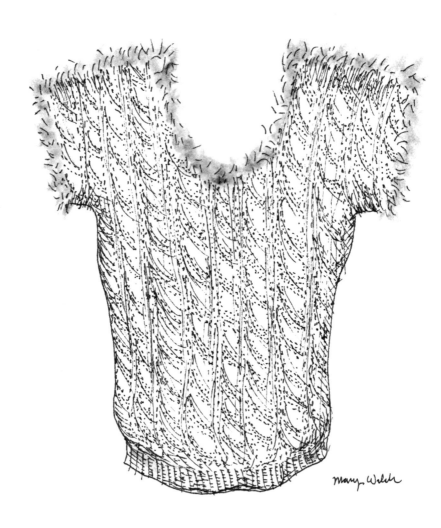

SILK OMBRÉ

ADVANCED LEVEL

DETAILS

Stitch	rib: knit 1, purl 1
	front: fan stitch
	back: stockinette
	trim: single crochet with picot edge
Gauge	stockinette: 6½ stitches, 7 rows/inch
Note	Scoop may be knit entirely in stockinette for a simpler version.

MATERIALS

1 skein	Sheepish Grin CS lavender ombré silk (800 yards)
1 ball	Melrose Belangor, mocha (angora)
	#2 knitting needles, 14″ long
	#5 knitting needles, 14″ long
	#6 knitting needles, 14″ long
	#5 crochet hook (size E)

DIRECTIONS

Back: With #2 needles and a single strand of ombré silk yarn, cast on 94 (100, 106) stitches. Work in rib pattern—knit 1, purl

1—for 1½ (2, 2) inches. Change to #6 needles and knit evenly in stockinette for 11 (12, 13) inches to armhole. Increase 1 stitch at either end of knit row, 2 (3, 3) times. Cast on 10 stitches at beginning of next 2 rows. Work for 1 inch. Bind off 14 stitches at center back. Work sleeve edge evenly as you work neck edge. For neck edge, decrease 1 stitch every row, 6 times. Continue evenly until stockinette section measures 18 (19, 20) inches long; bind off. **Front:** Repeat back rib pattern. Change to #5 needles; work 2 rows stockinette. Work remainder of front in fan stitch. *Fan Stitch:* see "Basic Stitchery: Fan Stitch." Work evenly in fan stitch for 11 (12, 13) inches*. Work cap-shape sleeve in same manner as back. *Neckline:* start ½ inch beyond cast-on sleeve stitches; bind off 14 stitches at center front. Shape neckline and sleeve same as back. Work until piece equals back length; bind off.

Finish: Sew side seams together. With crochet hook and angora yarn, work 1 row single crochet along front shoulder edge. Work 2nd row along back shoulder edge*. Seam shoulders together by joining first and second rows. Trim sleeves and neckline with 1 row single crochet, 1 row picot edge in angora yarn.

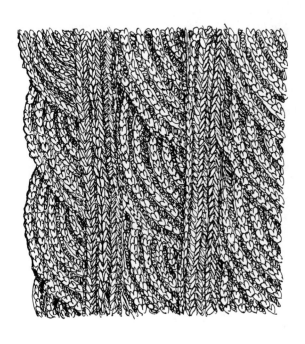
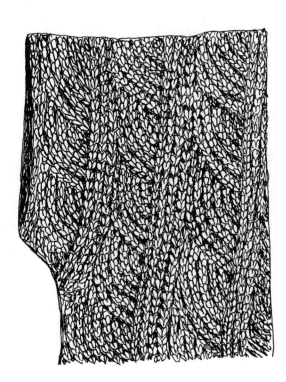

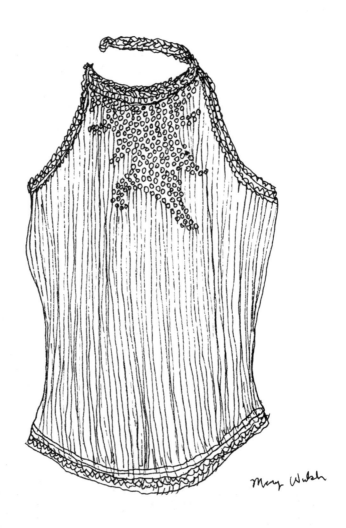

LAVA HALTER

BEGINNER LEVEL

DETAILS

Stitch   bodice: stockinette
            trim: single crochet
Gauge   5 stitches, 7 rows/inch
Notes   For decoration, beads may be sewn
            on; many presewn beaded appliqués
            are also available.

MATERIALS

4 skeins	Gemini Arielle #7671, black
6 skeins	Gemini Silkworm #1, black
1 skein	Melrose Cablenella, jet black
2 strings	gunmetal beads (optional)
1 yard	lace seam binding, ½" wide
1 yard	flat ⅜" elastic
	#7 circular knitting needle, 24" long
	#5 crochet hook (size E)
	button for neckline closure

DIRECTIONS

With #7 needle, 2 strands of Silkworm, and single strand of Arielle, cast on 152 (160, 168) stitches. Knit in the round for 9 (9½, 10) inches. **Back:** Bind off half of the stitches. **Front—** armhole: Bind off 4 stitches at beginning of next 2 rows. Decrease 1 stitch at beginning of every row to neckline. Starting 6½ (7, 7½) inches from armhole, bind off 20 stitches at center front; tie on yarn; knit across other side. Decrease 1 stitch at neck edge every other row. Work armhole edge straight until 3 stitches remain. Bind off.

Finish: With crochet hook and Cablenella, work 3 rows of single crochet along bottom edge, starting on inside. Work 3 rows along neckline edge; chain to extend 7 inches or proper length to fit around neck*(A). At end of 3rd row, add a buttonhole loop (5 chain stitches)*(B), then work 4th row back to armhole.

Armholes: Starting at neckline on inside edge and ending at underarm, work 3 rows of single crochet; connect to neckline as you work. Sew one side of lace seam binding to outside edge of back (see Pheasant Camisole). Fold toward inside; sew other edge to inside of back to form casing for elastic. Thread elastic through at open end; try on, cut elastic to proper fit, and sew in place. Sew a button at neckline for closure.

A

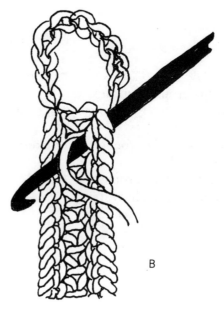

B

Leaf Halter

INTERMEDIATE LEVEL

DETAILS

Stitch	rib: knit 1, purl 1
	bodice: knit in the round; garter stitch; stockinette
	trim: crochet picot edge
	leaves: single, double, triple crochet
Gauge	8 stitches, 8½ rows/inch
Notes	Artificial leaves may replace crochet leaves. Dry, fresh, or artificial flowers would enhance the design as well.

MATERIALS

1 cone	DMC embroidery floss #3013, green
2 skeins	DMC embroidery floss #3012, green
12 skeins	DMC embroidery floss #94, green ombré
1 yard	round cotton batting, ½" thick
	#1 circular knitting needle, 24" long
	#3 circular knitting needle, 24" long
	#3 double-point knitting needles, 7" long
	#5 crochet hook (size E)
	large stitch holder

DIRECTIONS

With #1 needle and DMC #3013 yarn, cast on 216 (224, 232) stitches; tie ends together. Work rib stitch—knit 1, purl 1—for 1 inch. Change to #3 circular needle. Knit in the round for 10 (11, 12) inches. Place half of the stitches on holder (front); leave other half (back) on #3 needles. **Back:** Work 6 rows of garter stitch; bind off loosely. **Front:** Place half of front stitches on #3 needles. Work 3 garter stitches at either end of row and remainder in stockinette. Decrease both ends of knit rows until 12 stitches remain; Continue strap on #3 straight needles. continue plain stockinette for 15″ for strap*. Repeat procedure for other side; make this strap 18″ long.

Finish: Wrap knit straps around batting. Cut batting to size; slip-stitch closed. With crochet hook and single strand of #3012 green floss, work 1 single-crochet row and 1 picot edge row across hemline, 1 single-crochet row around top. *Leaves:* With double strand of green ombré floss, chain 10 stitches. Work 1 slip, 4 single, 3 double, then 7 triple crochet stitches in same space* (at the end of chain). Turn and work 2 double and 3 single stitches down other side of chain; end with slip stitch. Bind off. Attach about 18 to 20 leaves at random on straps and front.

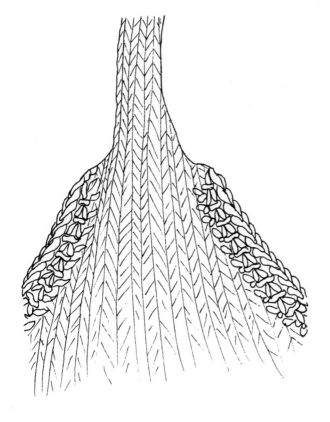

PHEASANT CAMISOLE

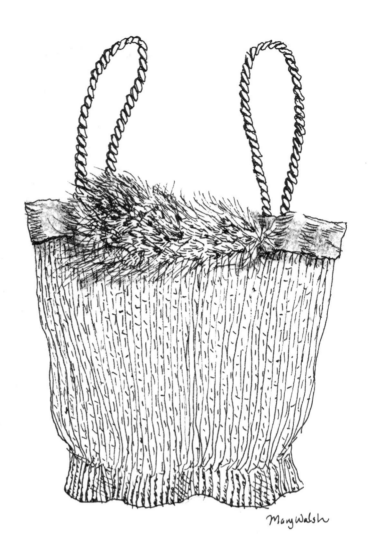

Mary Walsh

BEGINNER LEVEL

DETAILS

Stitch	rib: knit 1, purl 1
	bodice: knit in the round
Gauge	7 stitches, 8 rows/inch
Note	Optional trim could be feathers, silk flowers, or embroidery detail.

MATERIALS

1 skein	Scott's Mill silk tussah, sage green
2 rolls	Yarn Loft ⅛″ synthetic ribbon #73, sage green
1 yard	upholstery braid
1 yard	lace seam binding
1 yard	flat ⅜″ elastic
½ yard	grosgrain ribbon, 2″ wide, sage green
	#2 circular knitting needle, 24″ long
	#5 circular knitting needle, 24″ long

74

DIRECTIONS

With #2 needle and silk tussah yarn, cast on 176 (184, 192) stitches. Tie ends together; be careful not to twist stitches. Work rib stitch—knit 1, purl 1—for 2½ inches. Break yarn. Change to #5 needle, and tie in ribbon yarn at side seam. Work knit stitch in the round for 10 (11, 12) inches. Bind off loosely; weave in tails.

Finish: Cut braid to desired strap length. With straps hanging down, pin in place on outside at top edge; secure with zigzag stitch*(A). Sew one side of lace (over straps) to bind off camisole edge on outside*(B). Fold lace toward inside; press flat. Sew other lace edge to inside bodice to form casing for elastic*(C); leave open 1 inch. Cut elastic to your size and thread through casing; overlap raw ends; secure with zigzag stitch.

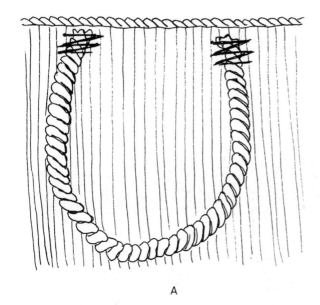

A

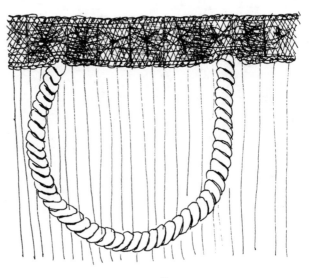

B

Slip-stitch casing closed. Press raw ends of grosgrain ribbon under ½ inch; sew one side of ribbon along top casing seam on inside*(D). Fold ribbon toward front; press; slip-stitch ribbon in place at sides. Apply feathers, flowers, or other suitable trim across front.

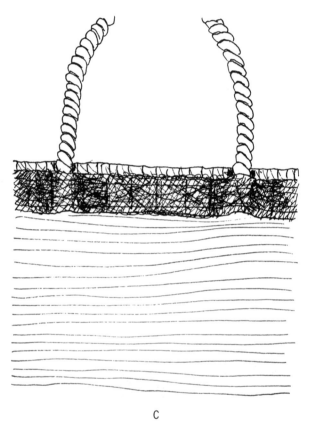

C

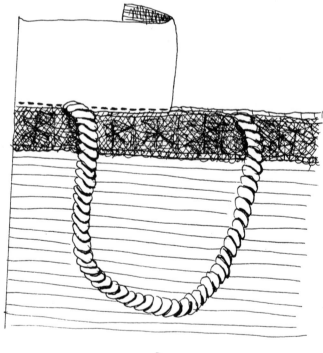

D

Cloud Camisole

Mary Walsh

INTERMEDIATE LEVEL

DETAILS

Stitch	rib: knit 1, purl 1 bodice: knit in the round trim: single crochet
Gauge	5 stitches, 7 rows/inch
Notes	If you tend to sneeze, mohair may be used instead of angora. Crystal drops or rhinestones are especially effective. The trapunto (puffy effect) for the cloud is optional.

MATERIALS

1 skein	Melrose Rayonette, gray
6 skeins	Unger Jewel #88, gray
1 ball	Unger Fluffy, gray
6	large crystal drops or rhinestones
12	small crystal drops or rhinestones
1 yard	narrow silver ribbon (¼″ or ½″ wide)

#1 circular knitting needle, 24″ long
#8 circular knitting needle, 24″ long
#5 crochet hook (size E)

DIRECTIONS

With #1 needle and Rayonette yarn, cast on 176 (184, 192) stitches. Tie ends together; work rib stitch—knit 1, purl 1—in the round for 2 inches. Cast off ribbing and set aside. With #8 needle and 2 strands of Jewel yarn, cast on 145 (152, 160) stitches. Knit in the round for 6 (7, 8) inches. Do not break yarn. (see Basic Equipment: Bobbins) Tie in Unger Fluffy 2½ (3, 3½) inches left of center; work according to cloud graph*. Tie on double strand of Jewel at other side of cloud; continue camisole. When cloud is complete, work in double strand of Jewel until 10 (11, 12) inches long; bind off.

Finish: Sew or crochet ribbing to bottom edge. With crochet hook and a single strand of Rayonette, work 3 rows of single crochet around top edge. Measure, pin, and sew ribbon straps to fit. Sew large crystal drops at random within cloud; sew small crystals "raining" down the front. Optional trapunto: Pin a small scrap of fabric to back of cloud; sew around cloud outline. Slit fabric from the back and stuff cloud section with cotton. Sew slit closed; this creates a puffed effect.

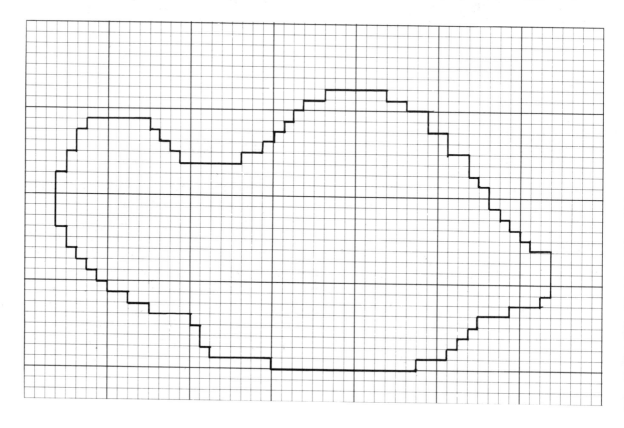

STAINED-GLASS CAMISOLE

INTERMEDIATE LEVEL

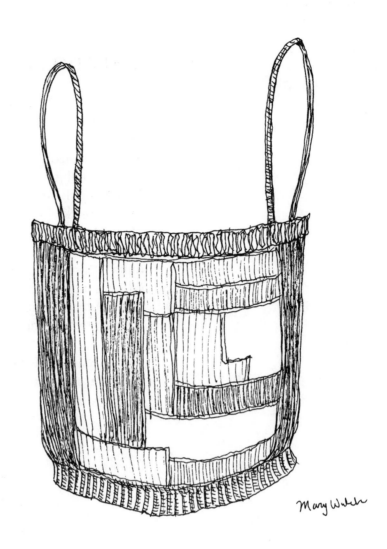

Mary Walker

DETAILS

Stitch	rib: moss stitch
	bodice: stockinette
Gauge	6½ stitches, 8½ rows/inch
Note	Metallic braid may be sewn on instead of knitting metallic yarn into pattern.

MATERIALS

3 skeins	Fantacia Paolino #169, black
1 skein	Fantacia Paolino #158, rose
1 skein	Fantacia Paolino #159, light purple
1 skein	Fantacia Paolino #164, aqua
1 skein	Fantacia Paolino #166, green
1 skein	Fantacia Paolino #160, dark purple
1 skein	Fantacia Paolino #162, blue
1 skein	Fantacia Metallic #1, pewter
1 yard	flat cord, black
	#2 knitting needles, 14″ long
	#5 knitting needles, 14″ long
3 packages	bobbins

DIRECTIONS

Back: With #2 needles and a single strand of black yarn, cast on 93 (99, 115) stitches. Work in moss stitch (see "Basic Stitchery: Moss Stitch")for 1½ inches. Change to #5 needles and work in stockinette stitch for 10½ (11½, 12½) inches. Change to #2 needles and work in moss stitch for 1 inch; bind off.

Front: (see Basic Equipment: Bobbins) Work rib in same manner as back. Change to #5 needles, work 6 (8, 12) rows in stockinette with black yarn before starting stained-glass design. Center design on front: small, 14 stitches either side; medium, 20 stitches; large, 26 stitches. Follow chart for colors, stitches, and rows*. Work 6 (8, 12) black stockinette rows until front bodice measures the same as back stockinette section. Change to #2 needles and work in moss stitch for 1 inch; bind off.

Finish: Sew camisole together at sides; weave in tails. Try on; measure, cut, pin, and sew straps in place on inside of top edge*.

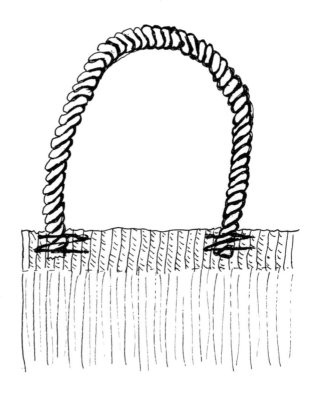

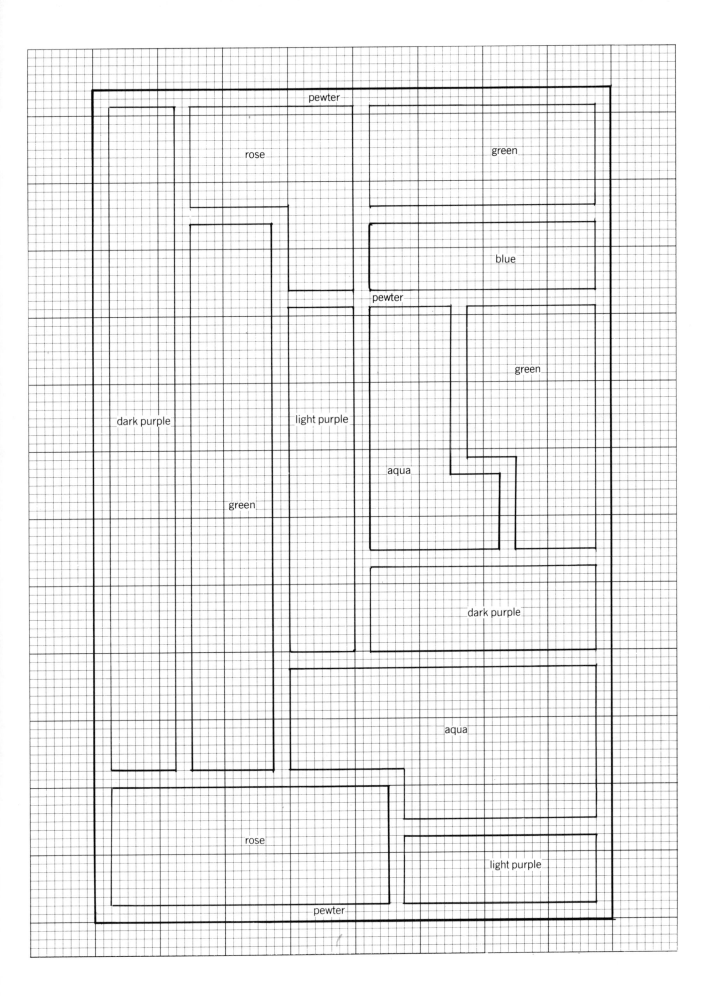

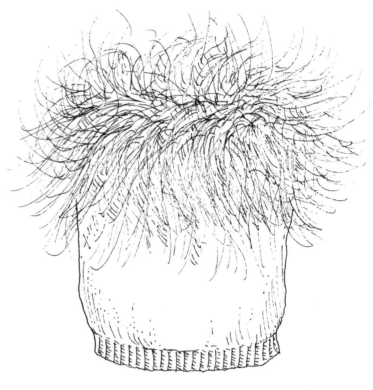

FEATHER BANDEAU

BEGINNER LEVEL

DETAILS

Stitch	rib: knit 1, purl 1
	bodice: knit in the round
Gauge	7 stitches, 8 rows/inch
Note	May be trimmed with ostrich feathers, marabou, or sequins.

MATERIALS

1 skein	Melrose Cravanella, white
1 spool	Yarn Lofts synthetic ribbon 01, white
1 yard	lace seam binding
1 yard	flat ⅜″ elastic
½ yard	satin ribbon, 2″ wide, white
½ yard	ostrich plumes (optional; available by yard or 6′ lengths)
	#2 circular knitting needle, 24″ long
	#5 circular knitting needle, 24″ long

DIRECTIONS

With #2 needle and Cravanella, cast on 176 (184, 192) stitches. Work rib stitch—knit 1, purl 1—for 1½ inches. Break yarn. Change to #5 needle and tie in synthetic ribbon. Knit in the round for 10 (11, 12) inches. Bind off loosely; weave in tails.

Finish: Sew lace to bind-off edge on outside of bandeau. Fold lace toward inside; press flat. Sew lace edge to inside bodice to form casing for elastic; leave open 1 inch. Cut elastic to your size and thread through casing. Overlap and sew raw ends of elastic together. Slip-stitch casing closed. Press raw ends of satin ribbon under ½ inch and sew ribbon along top casing seam on inside (see Pheasant Camisole). Fold ribbon toward front; press; slip-stitch ribbon at sides. Tack ostrich plumes or other decoration of your choice across front.

ROSE BANDEAU

INTERMEDIATE LEVEL

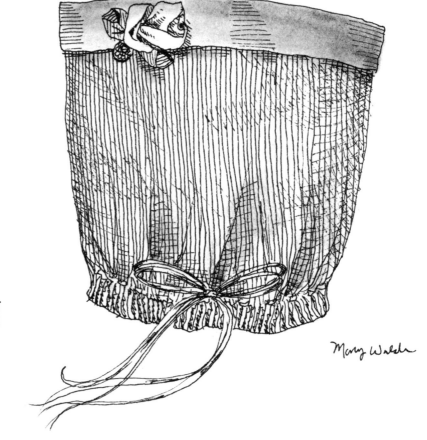

DETAILS

Stitch	rib: knit 1, purl 1
	bodice: knit in the round
Gauge	6 stitches, 8 rows/inch
Note	An artificial flower or appliqué may be used in place of the fabric flower.

MATERIALS

3 skeins	#3 DMC perle cotton #353, shrimp
3 skeins	Gemini Arielle #70, shrimp
1 yard	#3 DMC perle cotton #758, peach
½ yard	ombré ribbon 2″ wide (across front bodice)
1 package	lace seam binding
1 yard	flat ½″ elastic
2 yards	⅛ satin ribbon, pale shrimp
2 yards	⅛ satin ribbon, deep shrimp
	fabric scraps for flower (9″ × 3″)
¼ yard	grosgrain ribbon, ½″ wide, green
¼ yard	taffeta ribbon, 2″ wide, apricot

#2 circular knitting needle,
   24″ long
#5 circular knitting needle,
   24″ long
tapestry needle
knitting spool (optional)

DIRECTIONS

With #2 needle and a single strand of perle cotton, cast on 174 (186, 198) stitches. Work rib—knit 1, purl 1—for 1½ inches. Break yarn. Change to #5 needle and tie in a single strand of Arielle yarn. Knit in the round for 10 (11, 12) inches. Bind off loosely; weave in tails.

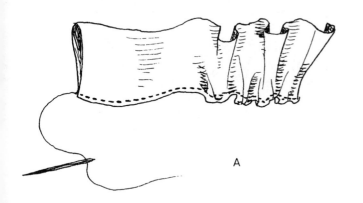

A

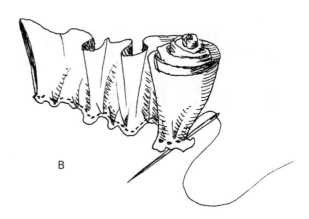

B

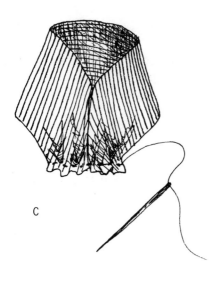

C

Finish: See Feather Bandeau. Weave both strands of narrow satin ribbon through Arielle with tapestry needle, and tie in bow at center of waist. *Flower:* Cut a scrap of fabric 9 inches long by 3 inches wide; fold in half lengthwise, and gather tightly along raw edges at bottom*(A). Fold raw edges in at sides and roll fabric around itself to create a flower. Roll tightly at center, loosely at outer edges*(B). Repeat procedure for taffeta ribbon and wrap around flower loosely; sew together at base. *Leaves:* Fold grosgrain ribbon into triangle, gather at base*(C). Pull together tightly to form leaf. *Stem:* With knitting spool and 1 yard peach perle cotton, work 3 inches (see Rosebud Lariat); bind off. Sew leaves and flower to one end of stem; curl other end under flower and sew entire piece to bandeau.

BUTTERFLY BANDEAU

INTERMEDIATE LEVEL

DETAILS

Stitch	rib: knit 1, purl 1
	bodice: knit in the round
Gauge	7 stitches, 8 rows/inch
Note	May be trimmed with needlework butterfly, sequins, or bead appliqué.

MATERIALS

4 skeins	DMC embroidery floss #3013, pale green
2 rolls	Yarn Loft ⅛″ synthetic ribbon #71, pale green
½ yard	moiré faille ribbon, 2″ wide, pale green
½ yard	antique gold fringe
1 yard	flat ⅜″ elastic
1 yard	lace seam binding
	#2 circular knitting needle, 24″ long
	#5 circular knitting needle, 24″ long

DIRECTIONS

Rib: With #2 needle and DMC floss, cast on 176 (184, 192) stitches. Tie ends together. Work rib—knit 1, purl 1—for 2½ inches. Break yarn. *Bodice:* Change to #5 needle and tie in a single strand of green ribbon. Knit in the round for 10 (11, 12) inches. Bind off loosely; weave in tails.

Finish: Sew lace seam binding to bind-off edge on outside of bandeau. Fold lace toward inside; press flat. Sew other lace edge to inside bodice to form casing for elastic; leave open 1 inch. Cut elastic to your size and thread through casing. Overlap raw ends; secure with zigzag stitch. Slip-stitch casing closed. Press raw ends of moiré ribbon under ½ inch and sew ribbon along top casing seam on inside (see Pheasant Camisole). Fold ribbon toward front, press; slip-stitch ribbon at sides. Sew optional metallic fringe to underside of ribbon. Apply needlework, sequins, or beaded appliqué.

Ruffled Wrap

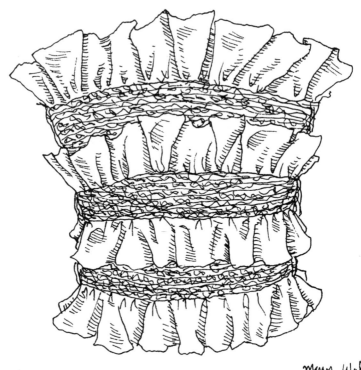

Mary Walsh

BEGINNER LEVEL

DETAILS

Stitch	stockinette
Gauge	5½ stitches, 6 rows/inch
Note	Fabric ruffles are shown. One size wraps to fit all, about 10″ wide at the bodice and 72″ long.

MATERIALS

2 skeins	Unger Angelspun #1106, cocoa
1 yard	taffeta, 45″ wide
2 packages	lace seam binding
	#5 knitting needles, 14″ long

DIRECTIONS

With #5 needles and single strand of Angelspun, cast on 4 stitches, and work in stockinette for 4 rows. On next row, increase 2 stitches at either end of knit row, 2 times. Continue to increase 1 stitch at either side every 6th knit row, 24 times;

use full fashion increase (see "Basic Stitchery: Knitting"). Work evenly for 20 inches. Decrease other side in same proportion to increase: 1 stitch either side every 6th knit row, 24 times. Bind off 2 stitches on either side of knit row, 2 times. Work 4 rows; bind off remaining 4 stitches.

Finish: Cut 3 strips of fabric (45″ × 6″) for ruffle. Sew ends together to create one long strip. Fold in half lengthwise, and steam-iron along fold. With large gathering stitches, sew along raw edges; pull stitches to gather fabric*. Adjust length of fabric ruffle to equal circumference of wrap; pin and sew in place on right side of wrap, along edges. Slip-stitch ruffle ends together. Sew one side of lace binding to right side of wrap, over raw edge of ruffles. Turn and press binding to inside; sew other edge of lace to inside. Try on, and sew hooks and eyes at ends of wrap for proper fit. If you want a snug fit, thread narrow elastic through lace seam binding and secure ends. Try on for proper fit. Sew on fasteners. May also be worn as a shawl or scarf.

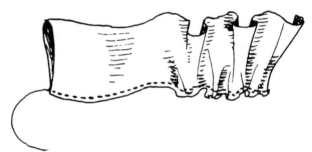

ALTERNATE MACHINE INSTRUCTIONS by Carolyn Dadisman

Machine: Brother 230 (bulky machine)
Stitch size 2
Gauge: 5½ stitches, 6 rows/inch

DIRECTIONS

Follow directions for hand knit, except: Cast on (with e-wrap) 4 stitches. Increase 2 stitches (e-wrap) 1 time on each side. Then continue to increase 1 stitch at either side every 6th knit row, 24 times. Start on Row 10, 154 stitches. Knit straight to row 270. Then decrease 1 stitch every 6th row, 24 times. This brings you to row 414. Knit 6 more rows, binding off 2 stitches on either side of knit row and then remaining 4 stitches on last row.

BUTTERFLY WRAP

ADVANCED LEVEL

DETAILS

Stitch	wrap: stockinette
	butterfly: single crochet; crochet shell stitch
Gauge	8 stitches, 10–11 rows/inch
Notes	Butterfly is embellished with sequins, beads, and metallic threads; substitute bright-colored yarns for day wear. May be appliquéd to any garment. One size wraps to fit all, about 10″ wide at center and 72″ long.

MATERIALS

3 skeins	Unger Allure #904, black #909,
1 skein	brown
1 skein	Unger Ariane #19, gold
1 skein	Unger Ariane #16, copper
small portion	cotton stuffing
1 yard	each of assorted sequins (optional)
1 package	copper beads
	#5 knitting needles, 14″ long
	#5 double-pointed knitting needles, 7″ long
	#5 crochet hook (size E)
	wire

DIRECTIONS

With #5 needles and single strand of black Allure, cast on 4 stitches, and work in stockinette 4 rows. On next knit row increase 2 stitches at both ends; repeat on next 2 knit rows. Continue to increase 1 stitch both ends of every knit row, 5 times. Thereafter increase 1 stitch both ends every 8th knit row, 35 times; use a full fashion increase. Work evenly for 20 inches. Decrease other side in same proportion to increase: 1 stitch both ends, every 8th knit row, 35 times. Then 1 stitch both ends every knit row, 5 times. Then 2 stitches both ends of knit row, 2 times. Knit 4 rows; bind off remaining 4 stitches.

Edge: With crochet hook and single strand of black Allure, work 2 rows of single crochet around entire edge of wrap; 1st row is worked from outside, and 2nd row is worked from inside. Try on and sew hooks and eyes at end of wrap for proper fit.

Butterfly body*: With #5 double-pointed knitting needles and single strand of brown and of copper, cast on 14 stitches. Work evenly in stockinette for 4 inches. Change yarns to single strand of black Allure and single strand of copper. Decrease 1 stitch at either end of each knit row every 1½ inches, until piece measures 10 inches long. Bind off remaining 6 stitches. Sew edges together and stuff with cotton to form a body. Slip-stitch opening closed. String copper beads on thin wire for antennae; sew to top center of body.

Butterfly wings*: *Section 1:* With crochet hook and single strand of black and of brown, chain 25 stitches. Work in single crochet stitch for 10 rows. Thereafter decrease 1 stitch every other row on outside edge of wing, 5 times. Crochet 6 more rows; decrease 5 stitches every other row on outside edge until 5 stitches remain. Work 1 row along straight inside edge; bind off. *Section 2:* With single strand of copper and of brown, work 3 rows of single crochet from point A to point B; work 2 stitches at corners. *Section 3:* With 2 strands of copper, work 5 rows of single crochet from A, back to A. Work 6th row from A to C, 7th row to D, 8th row to E. *Section 4:* With single strand of copper and of gold, work 3 rows of single crochet back and forth, to and from A. Work 4th row to E, and continue row with 5 shell stitches. *Section 5:* With single strand of gold, work 3 rows of single crochet around entire wing. Repeat procedure for other wing. Pin body and wing sections to center front of

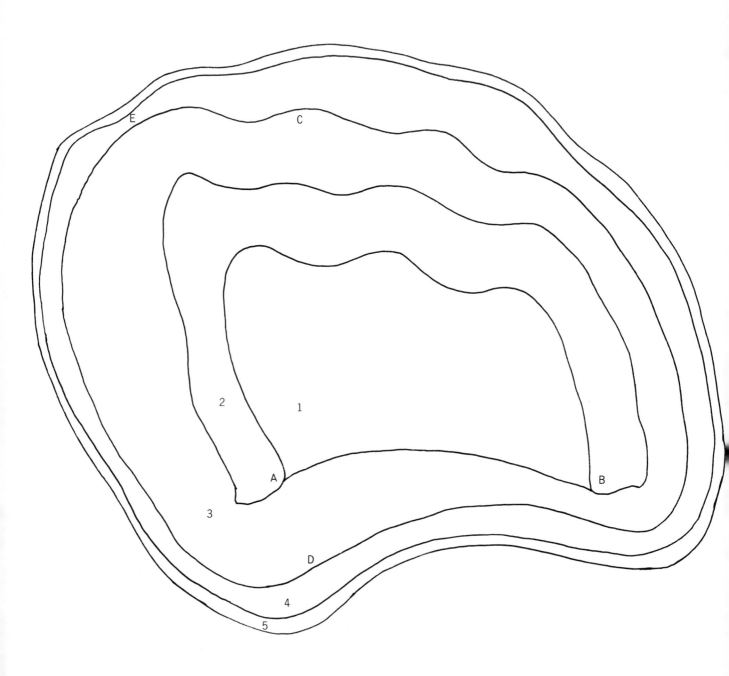

wrap. Try on and adjust placement; sew securely in place at several strategic spots from the inside of wrap, or use as an appliqué on a ready-to-wear ensemble. Sew 3 or 4 different-colored sequins in center of top and bottom wing sections with sewing thread.

ALTERNATE MACHINE INSTRUCTIONS by Carolyn Dadisman

Machine: Bulky 8 machine

Stitch size 7
Gauge: 8 stitches, 10.9 rows/inch

DIRECTIONS

Follow directions for hand knit, except: Cast on (with e-wrap) 4 stitches. Increase 2 stitches (e-wrap) 1 time on each side. Then increase 1 stitch (e-wrap) 1 time on each side. Increase a total of 10 stitches in 6 rows. Continue to increase 1 stitch every 8th knit row, 35 times. Start on row 8 (use full fashion increase or decrease); last increase is on row 280. Knit straight to row 494. Then decrease 1 stitch every 8th knit row, 35 times. Last decrease is on row 766. Bind off 1 stitch each side at row 770. Bind off 2 stitches each side at row 772. Bind off remaining 4 stitches at row 774.

SHORT-SLEEVED JACKET

INTERMEDIATE LEVEL

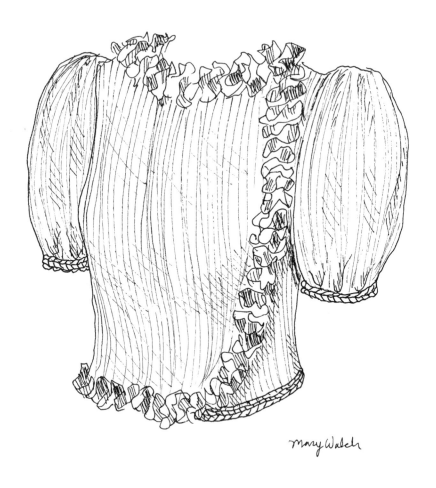

Mary Walsh

DETAILS

Stitch	bodice: stockinette trim: single crochet
Gauge	6 stitches, 7 rows/inch
Note	Crochet trim and ruffles make hem full and wide; if you prefer a more tailored look, a knit 1, purl 1 rib can be used instead.

MATERIALS

10 skeins	Gemini Silkworm #2, white
8 skeins	Gemini Mirage #0, white
2 rolls	Gemini Petite Starlight #8894, white
1 roll	Mokuba Organdy #2, white
	#7 knitting needles, 14" long
	#5 crochet hook (size E)
	large tapestry needle

DIRECTIONS

Back: With #7 needles, 1 strand of Silkworm, and 1 strand of Mirage, cast on 100 (108, 116) stitches. Work evenly in stockinette stitch for 10 (10½, 11) inches to armhole. Bind off 4 stitches at beginning of next 2 rows. Full fashion decrease 1 stitch, every other row, 7 times. Work evenly until armhole measures 7 (7½, 8) inches to neckline. Bind off 24 stitches at center back; tie on yarn; full fashion decrease 1 stitch at neck edge every other row, 6 times; then decrease every row, 3 times. Bind off. **Right front:** Cast on 62 (70, 78) stitches. To shape curve, increase 1 stitch at beginning of every knit row, 10 times. Work evenly until front is 10 (10½, 11) inches to armhole. Bind off 4 stitches at beginning of purl row. Full fashion decrease 1 stitch at armhole edge every purl row, 6 times. Work evenly until armhole measures 5½ (6, 6½) inches to front neckline. Knit 12 (14, 16) stitches; tie on yarn; bind off 22 (24, 26) stitches; continue to knit across the row. Full fashion decrease 1 stitch at neck edge every other row, 7 times. Continue armhole evenly; work until front armhole is same length as back armhole. Bind off at shoulder. Work narrow side of front neckline in the same manner: Decrease at neck, keep side even, bind off at shoulder. **Left front:** Cast on 46 (54, 62) stitches. Work evenly for 10 (10½, 11) inches to armhole. Bind off 4 stitches at beginning of knit row. Full fashion decrease 1 stitch every knit row, 6 times. Work evenly until armhole measures 5½ (6, 6½) inches. Bind off 12 stitches at beginning of purl row; full fashion decrease 1 stitch at neck edge every other row, 7 times. Work evenly until armhole equals back armhole. Bind off at shoulder. **Sleeves:** Cast on 90 (98, 106) stitches, work evenly for 4½ (5, 5½) inches. Bind off 5 stitches at beginning of next 2 rows; full fashion decrease 1 stitch either end every other row, 3 times. Continue evenly for 6 (6½, 7) inches. Decrease 1 stitch either end of every row, 4 times. To gather, knit 2 stitches together across the row; repeat on purl row. Knit 1 plain row, bind off on next row.

Finish: Weave in tails; block pieces and sew together. Trim: With crochet hook and a single strand of Petite Starlight, work 3 rows of single crochet stitch. Start at side seam and work from the inside edges. Work 1 continuous row around the hem, front, and neckline. Bind off. Gather the sleeves by working every other stitch at the bottom inside edge, for the first row of crochet. Continue with 2 more rows of single crochet. *Ruffle trim*: With crochet hook and white Organdy knitting tape, work large loops along knit edge of right front. Work one loop in between each crochet trim stitch, close together, to create ruffles. Start at side seam; pull tape through to inside with crochet hook and hold each loop in place with a single small sewing stitch with tapestry needle and a strand of Mirage. A second roll of Organdy may be used to ruffle around the entire hem, making it stand out even farther.

LONG-SLEEVED JACKET

INTERMEDIATE LEVEL

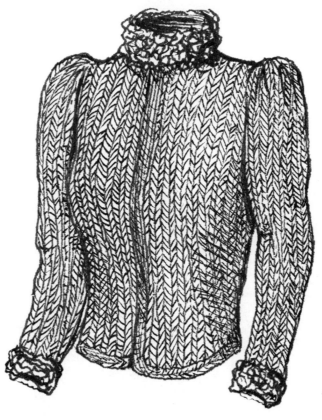

Mary Walsh

DETAILS

Stitch	bodice: stockinette
	trim: single crochet
Gauge	4 stitches, 6 rows/inch
Note	Jacket shown with detachable collar and cuffs, which are worked separately and may be worn as an accessory for other jackets as well.

MATERIALS

10 skeins	Fantacia Pangra #2964, mauve
	#8 knitting needles, 14″ long
	#5 crochet hook (size E)

DIRECTIONS

Back: With #8 knitting needles and a single strand of Pangra, cast on 58 (64, 70) stitches. Work in stockinette stitch for 12 (13,

14) inches to armhole. Bind off 2 stitches at the beginning of next 2 rows. Decrease 1 stitch either end every other row, 2 times. Use full fashion decrease method. Continue evenly until 6½ (7, 7½) inches above armhole. Bind off 10 stitches at center back for neckline. Tie on yarn. Decrease 1 stitch at neck edge every other row, 1 (2, 3) times. Bind off at shoulder. **Front:** Cast on 38 (42, 46) stitches. Work in stockinette for 12 (13, 14) inches to armhole. Bind off 3 stitches at beginning of next row. Full fashion decrease 1 stitch at armhole edge every other row, 3 times. Continue evenly until 6½ (7, 7½) inches above armhole. Bind off 4 (6, 8) stitches for neckline. Decrease 1 stitch at neckline edge every row, 12 times. Bind off at shoulder. Repeat for other side of front, being sure to reverse the shape of armhole and neckline. **Sleeves:** Cast on 36 (40, 44) stitches; increase 1 stitch either end every 8th row, 8 times; then every 6th row, 3 times. *Armhole:* Bind off 4 stitches at beginning of next 2 rows. Decrease 1 stitch either end every row, 4 times; then every other row, 2 times; then every 3rd row, 8 times; then every row, 3 times. Bind off 3 stitches at beginning of next 2 rows; then 4 stitches on next 2 rows, then remaining stitches.

Finish: Block, and weave in tails. Weave seams at shoulder; sew sleeves to bodice sections, then sew underarm seams and bodice side seams. *Trim:* With crochet hook and a single strand of Pangra, work 3 rows of single crochet (from inside edge) around cuff, hem, center front, and neckline edges. These may be worked in continuous rows, working 2 stitches in 1 loop to turn the corners (at top and bottom of center front opening). If you choose to add buttons, crochet a 4th row on the center front, using the picot stitch to create button loops.

COLLAR AND CUFFS

DETAILS

Stitch	reverse stockinette
Gauge	4 stitches, 6 rows/inch
Note	Collar and cuffs for the long-sleeved jacket may be substituted by fur, feathers, or other purchased trim.

MATERIALS

2 skeins	Fantacia Serenade #861, taupe, rust, smoke (tri-color yarn)
1 package	large hooks and eyes
	#8 knitting needles, 10" long
	#5 crochet hook (size E)

DIRECTIONS

Collar: With #8 needles and a single strand of Serenade, cast on 72 stitches. Work evenly in reverse stockinette for 3¼ inches. Cast off.

Cuffs: Cast on 40 stitches. Work evenly for 3½ inches in reverse stockinette. Cast off. Work second cuff in the same manner as the first.

Finish: With crochet hook and a single strand of Serenade, work a row of single crochet around entire edge. Block. Sew hooks and eyes at either ends of cuffs and at center front of collar. Slip over sleeves and around neck of long-sleeved jacket.

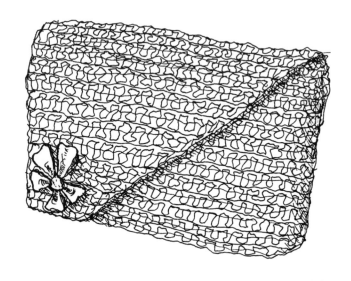

May Welch

RIBBON CLUTCH

BEGINNER LEVEL

DETAILS

Stitch	single crochet
Gauge	4 stitches, 2 rows/inch
Notes	A combination of fibers (ribbon and yarn left over from a sweater) works well as a coordinate. A forlorn earring or shoe buckle make a great decorative closure.

MATERIALS

3 skeins   Anny Blatt Serpentine #1409–5739, pewter and gold (bicolor yarn)
#10 crochet hook (size J)
decorative closure (covered snap or Velcro)

DIRECTIONS

With crochet hook and a single strand of yarn, chain 32 stitches. Turn and work rows back and forth in single crochet stitch. Crochet evenly until purse measures 10 inches long. Then decrease at inside edge every row, until 10 stitches remain; bind off.

Finish: Weave in tails; fold rectangular portion of purse in half* (slanted portion becomes front flap). Seam clutch sides together with one row of single crochet, worked on outside, beginning on lower edge. Fold over flap and sew on snap, or Velcro closure. Decorate with buckle, button, or pin sewed to the corner of top flap.

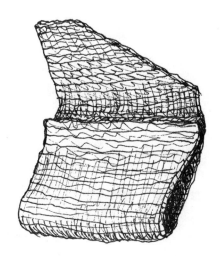

TASSELED PURSE

BEGINNER LEVEL

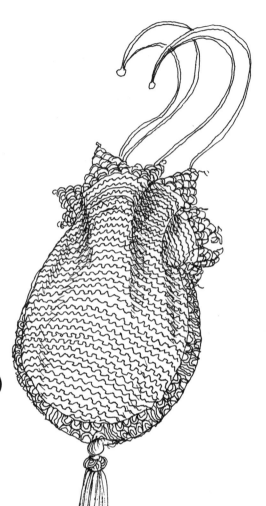

DETAILS

Stitch   garter
Gauge   6 stitches, 5 rows/inch
Note   Antique lace was used in
            example; however, ribbon,
            fabric, or other trim are equally
            effective. Or you can
            crochet the lace
            sections in
            a fine yarn.

MATERIALS

2 rolls	Gemini ¼″ ombré ribbon #107, écru
¾ yard	flat-edged lace, 2″ wide
¾ yard	picot-edged lace, 1½″ wide
1 package	small plastic rings
2 yards	cording
1	tassel, 12″ long
	#7 knitting needles, 10″ long
	Tacky glue

DIRECTIONS

Front: Work entire purse in garter stitch. With #7 needles and ribbon, cast on 20 stitches. From the start, increase 1 stitch either end of even rows, 12 times (until 44 stitches are on needle). Work evenly until piece measures 9″; bind off. **Back:** Repeat above procedure.

Finish: Sew flat-edged lace between 2 purse sections, along sides, and across bottom*. Sew picot-edged lace along top edge. Sew 10 small rings to inside of purse, 2 inches apart, 1½ inches from top edge. Cut cording in half and thread through rings; thread 1 cord from each side for drawstring*. Tie raw ends of cord; cut close, and secure with Tacky glue. Sew long tassel to center of bottom from the inside.

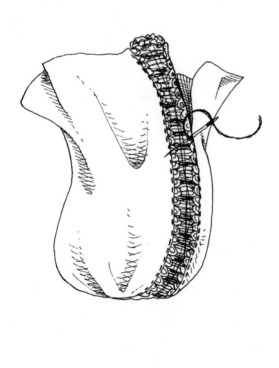

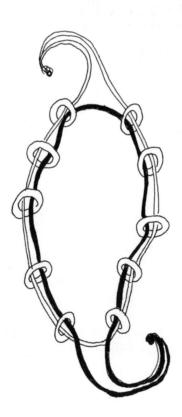

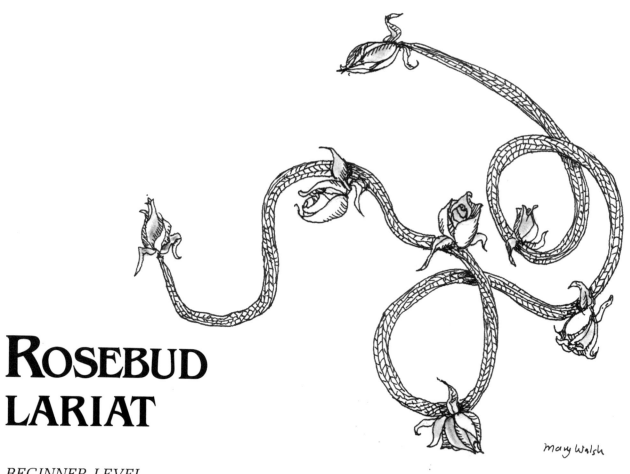

ROSEBUD
LARIAT

BEGINNER LEVEL

DETAILS

Stitch	knitting spool
Gauge	approximately 10 yards (becomes 32″ long when knit through spool)
Note	May be used as neck ring, belt, hairpiece, hatband, bracelet, or even a purse handle (thread a shoelace through the center of knitted tube for strength).

MATERIALS

1 skein	light green silk twist, or #3 DMC perle cotton #472
1 skein	medium green silk twist, or #3 DMC perle cotton #471
1 skein	deep green silk twist, or #3 DMC perle cotton #470
1 dozen	dry or artificial rosebuds and leaves
	knitting spool
	Tacky glue
	#3 crochet hook (size C)
	tapestry needle

DIRECTIONS

Thread a single strand of light green yarn from the top through the center hole of knitting spool; strand should extend several inches from the bottom. Wrap top yarn 2 times *around* each nail*. Loop lower strand over upper strand and off the nail with crochet hook to create a stitch; work 1 nail at a time. Hereafter wrap yarn on *outside* of nail. Lay yarn above previous stitch and continue to loop lower strand over upper strand, thereby knitting in the round. Pull on extended bottom yarn frequently to keep tension even. Work light green yarn to end; tie on medium green, tucking yarn tails into center of tube, and continue to end of medium shade. Tie on deep green, and work in the same manner to within a 5-inch tail. Thread yarn end with tapestry needle and slip through last 4 stitches on knitting spool, slip off nail, and sew end closed.

Finish: Glue rosebuds at random along knit tube and at either end. (Tacky glue is advised.) Add silk, velvet, or paper leaves from the florist. Or you may choose to add crochet leaves (see Leaf Halter) or ribbon leaves (see Rose Bandeau).

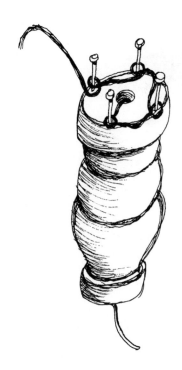

SABLE-TAIL LARIAT

BEGINNER LEVEL

DETAILS

Stitch	stockinette
Gauge	8 stitches, 8 rows/inch (may be made wider or shorter)
Notes	Lariat may be worn diagonally over one shoulder, double-wrapped at the neck, or as a long necklace. It is approximately 1″ round and 54″ long.

MATERIALS

1 skein	#3 DMC perle cotton #839, dark brown
1 skein	#3 DMC perle cotton #841, medium brown
1 skein	#3 DMC perle cotton #842, light brown
1½ yards	round cording, ½″ thick
1 yard each	3 or 4 novelty yarns for wrapping, fur scraps, or choice of optional decorations
	#5 double-pointed knitting needles, 7″ long

DIRECTIONS

With #5 needles and a single strand of dark brown yarn, cast on 12 stitches. Work evenly in stockinette to end of skein. Tie on medium brown yarn, and work to end of skein; repeat with light brown yarn, and bind off at end of skein. Lariat will be approximately 54″ long, ¾″ wide.

Finish: Wrap lariat around cording and pin sides together at back. Sew seam closed with matching thread; sew ends together to form a circle*. Wrap novelty yarns around each different-colored section and secure the tails under back seam with small stitches. (Optional): Sew on fur scraps or, if you prefer, small twisted hanks of your favorite yarn, or a large decorative accessory, at each color change, using the lariat as a charm necklace.

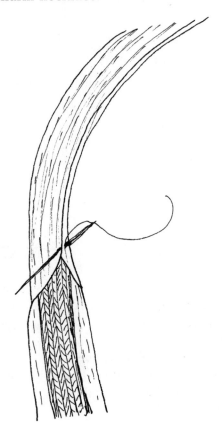

IVORY SHAWL

BEGINNER LEVEL

DETAILS

Stitch	garter
Gauge	4–6 stitches, 3–4 rows/inch (approximate, with different yarns)
Notes	Any yarns may be used for a mixed-media effect; 7 varieties of yarn were used here, in 8 different tones. The subtle gradation makes a sophisticated design.

MATERIALS

A number of scrap yarns were used. Yarns were worked in the following order and length in which they were stitched:

    mohair, white, 12"
    ribbon, white, 7"
    mohair mix, white, 7"
    mohair, white, 3½"
    cording, ivory, 5"
    angora, ivory, 10"
    bouclé, ivory, 11"
    ribbon, écru, 9"
    silk, écru, 8"
    #13 knitting needles, 14" long
    optional decorations

DIRECTIONS

With #13 needles and darkest tone, cast on 60 stitches. Work from deep to light tones to keep yarn clean. Work evenly in garter stitch. Shawl measures approximately 24″ wide and 72″ long. Bind off loosely at end of last section. Optional effects add finesse to the finish. Consider foxtails or fur scraps for ends, yarn fringe, random knots, or yarn tassels.

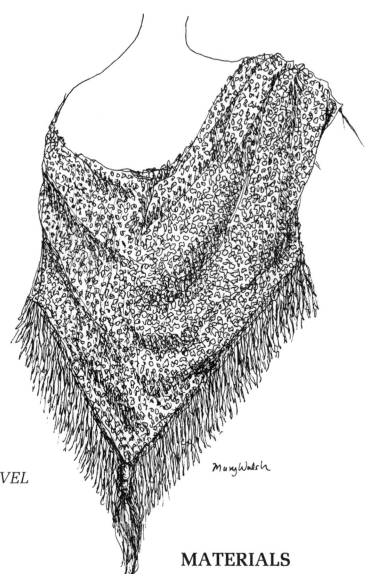

BLACK SHAWL

INTERMEDIATE LEVEL

DETAILS

Stitch	lace knit
Gauge	100 stitches/18 inches long
Notes	Knit loosely for open lace effect. Keep tension even; pull work down from needle while working. Try weaving ribbon of the same or contrast color through the stitches (all over or at the edges).

MATERIALS

2 skeins	Melrose Cravanella, black
4 skeins	Gemini Silkworm, black
2½ yards	black fringe, 6″ long
2½ yards	black upholstery braid, ½″ wide
1 large	black tassel, 6″ long
	#13 circular knitting needle, 24″ long

110

DIRECTIONS

Start shawl at the bottom center; with #13 needle, single strand of Cravanella, and 2 strands of Silkworm, cast on 4 stitches. Work lace stitch in following manner: 1st row; knit across; 2nd row; knit 1, yarn over, knit 2 together; repeat across the row. Add 1 stitch either end of knit row throughout. Work to create a triangle approximately 36–38″ long (from center point to bind-off edge). Cast off loosely.

Finish: Sew braid to top of fringe. Then sew fringe along 2 sides of triangle; leave bind-off edge plain. Sew long tassel at center back point.

Mary Walsh

SHELL NECKLACE

INTERMEDIATE LEVEL

DETAILS

Stitch   knitting spool
Gauge   approximately 10 yards/ (becomes
          32″ long when knit through spool)
Note   Experiment with various color com-
          binations. Try bright colors or wrap-
          ping with metallic fibers. A great way
          to make a coordinate accessory by
          using some leftover yarn from a pre-
          vious sweater.

MATERIALS

1 large   shell slice
1 skein   #3 DMC perle cotton, écru
1 skein   #5 DMC perle cotton #712, cream
1 skein   #5 DMC perle cotton #739, pale
           apricot
1 skein   #5 DMC perle cotton #951, pale
           peach
1 skein   DMC embroidery floss, écru
1 yard   narrow cable cord
           knitting spool
           #3 crochet hook (size C)
           tapestry needle
           Tacky glue

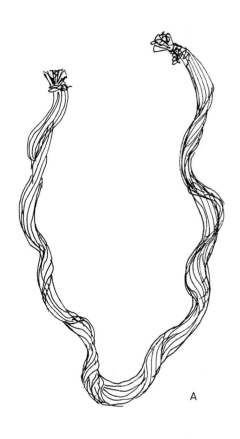

A

DIRECTIONS

With knitting spool and crochet hook, work écru perle cotton to end of skein (see Rosebud Lariat); leave end open. Dip raw end of cable cord into glue and let dry. Thread cord through the center of knit tube. Sew ends of tube together to form a circle. Divide circle into thirds; mark with pins. Untwist and cut through each skein of perle cotton at the knot; tie each set of loose ends with an 8″-long sewing thread*(A). Start with cream at first pin and loosely wrap skein around tube to second pin*(B). Secure loose ends of #5 perle by tying sewing thread to tube. Clip threads close. Repeat wrap-and-tie procedure for pale apricot from second pin to third pin, pale peach from third pin to first pin.

Finish: At points 1, 2, and 3, where ends are tied together, wrap each section with a double strand of écru embroidery floss several times and secure in place by pulling tapestry needle through cord. Cut raw ends close; tuck under wraps*(C). Hang shell from point 2 at center front with double strands of écru embroidery floss wrapped in same manner.

B

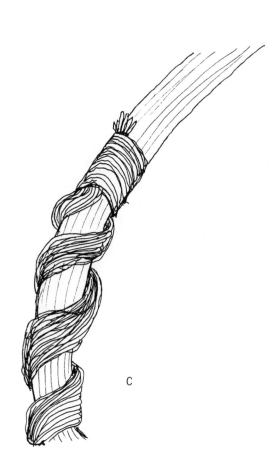

C

Mary Welch

FLORAL BELT

ADVANCED LEVEL

DETAILS

Stitch	knit: stockinette
	embroidery: threaded running, lazy daisy, French knot, bullion
Gauge	6 stitches, 8 rows/inch
Note	May be worn as a belt, necklace, or hatband. Try it with a black background and bright-colored flowers, or use beads in lieu of embroidery.

MATERIALS

1 ball	DMC crochet cotton, écru
1 skein	DMC embroidery floss #3053, pale green
1 skein	#3051 green
1 skein	#3042, pale lavender
1 skein	#3041, lavender
1 skein	#3078, pale yellow
1 skein	#225, pale pink
1 skein	#224, pink
1 skein	#223, rose
1 yard	heavy cable cord, ½″ thick
	#5 double-pointed knitting needles, 7″ long
	tapestry needle
	embroidery needle
	Tacky glue

114

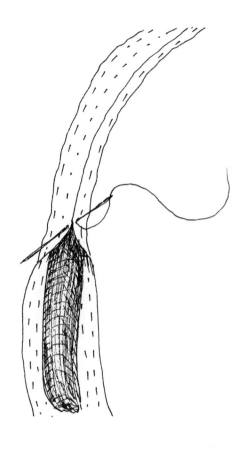

DIRECTIONS

With #5 knitting needles and single strand of écru crochet cotton, cast on 12 stitches. Work evenly in stockinette until length measures 1 inch less than waist size; bind off. **Embroidery;** *Vines* and *leaves:* With embroidery needle and green floss, work step 1 of threaded running stitch. With pale green floss, work step 2, creating vines along length of belt*(A). With green and pale green, work several leaves in lazy daisy stitch at random along vines. *Flowers:* With pale lavender at inside and lavender at outside, work several French knots in a circle with 1 large knot in pale yellow at the center; place at random*(B). With rose floss and small lazy daisy stitches, add 7 to 9 rosebuds to vines. With pale pink and 3 small bullion stitches, work center of flower; with pink and 2 large bullion stitches, work outside of flower; scatter 6 to 9 roses along vines*(C).

Finish: Center cord on wrong side of needlework; with tapestry needle and a single strand of yarn, stitch belt closed around cord; taper at either end. Thread 3 strands of yarn approximately 50 inches long through each end; fold in half to make 6 strands. Divide yarn into thirds, and braid for ties 12–15 inches long. Knot at ends, cut close, and secure with glue.

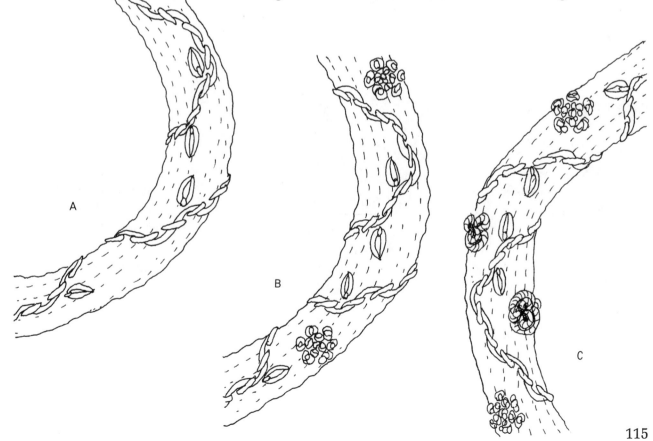

A

B

C

RETAIL AND WHOLESALE SUPPLIERS

RETAIL YARN

CALIFORNIA

CARMEL NEEDLEWORKS
Lincoln between 5th and 6th
P.O. Box 3383
Carmel, CA 93921
(408) 624-8475

CONNECTICUT

HOOK AND NEEDLE
1869 Post Road East
Westport, CT 06880
(203) 259-5119

THIMBLES
43 William Street
Greenwich, CT 06830
(203) 661-9266

THE YARN BASKET
1482 Post Road
Fairfield, CT 06430
(203) 255-5689

GEORGIA

STRINGS AND STRANDS
4632 Wieuca Road
Atlanta, GA 30342
(404) 252-9662

MASSACHUSETTS

NANTUCKET WOOL GATHERER
13 Center Street
Nantucket, MA 02554
(617) 228-5800

NEW YORK

COULTER STUDIOS
118 East 59th Street
New York, NY 10022
(212) 421-8085

GEMINI INNOVATIONS, LTD.
720 East Jericho Turnpike
Huntington Station, NY 11746
(516) 549-5650
(wholesale and retail)

WHOLESALE YARN

CALIFORNIA

FANTACIA
415 East Beach Avenue
Inglewood, CA 90302

CONNECTICUT

WILLIAM UNGER YARNS
P.O. Box 1621
Bridgeport, CT 06601
(203) 335-5000; 1-800-223-7526

MICHIGAN

LAINES ANNY BLATT
24770 Crestview Court
Farmington Hills, MI 48018
(313) 474-2942

NEW JERSEY

DMC
107 Trumbull Street
Elizabeth, NJ 07206
(201) 351-4550

SHEEPISH GRIN
40 Fairfield Road
Kingston, NJ 08528
(609) 924-YARN

TAHKI IMPORTS, LTD.
92 Kennedy Street
Hackensack, NJ 07601
(201) 489-9505

NEW YORK

MELROSE YARN COMPANY
1305 Utica Avenue
Brooklyn, NY 11203
(718) 629-0200;
1-800-MEL-YARN

UTAH

YARN LOFTS INTERNATIONAL
45 West 300 North
Provo, Utah 84601
(801) 377-3900

WASHINGTON

SCANDINAVIAN HOUSE IMPORTS
P.O. Box 99268
Tacoma, WA 98499
(206) 475-3714

NOTIONS

M & J TRIMMING CO.
1008 Sixth Avenue
New York, NY 10018
(212) 391-9072
(retail)

SHERU
29 West 37th Street
New York, NY 10018
(212) 944-6980
(retail and wholesale)

ASSOCIATIONS AND SCHOOLS

UNITED STATES

THE KNITTING GUILD
P.O. Box 1606
Knoxville, TENN 37901
(615) 524-2401

SOCIETY OF CRAFT DESIGNERS
Mr. Jim Miller
Box 7741
Columbus, GA 31908

CANADA

CRUCCI SCHOOL OF KNITTING
2 Pemperance Street
Toronto, Canada M5H 1Y4

BIBLIOGRAPHY

INSTRUCTION

Colton, Virginia, ed. *Reader's Digest Complete Guide to Needlework.* Pleasantville, NY: Reader's Digest Association, 1979.

Elalouf, Sion. *The Knitting Architect.* California: Knitting Fever, 1982. Roosevelt, NY: 11575

Gostelow, Mary. *The Complete Guide to Needlework Techniques and Materials.* Secaucus, NJ: Chartwell Books, 1982.

Hurlbutt, Regina. *Left Handed Crochet.* NY: Van Nostrand Reinhold Company, 1978.

Hurlbutt, Regina. *Left Handed Knitting.* NY: Van Nostrand Reinhold Company, 1977

Read, Susannah, ed. *The Needleworker's Constant Companion.* NY: Studio Book/Viking Press, 1978.

INFORMATION

Righetti, Maggie. *Universal Yarn Finder.* Vols. I, II. Atlanta, Ga: Maggie Righetti Designs, 1983, 1984.

EXPLORATION

Fiber Arts Magazine. *The Fiberarts Design Books.* Vols. I, II. N. Car.: Lark Books, 1983.

INSPIRATION

Kranz, Stewart, and Robert Fisher. *The Design Continuum.* NY: Van Nostrand Reinhold Company, 1966.

Larson, Jack Lenor, and Mildred Constantine. *The Art Fabric: Mainstream.* NY: Van Nostrand Reinhold Company.

Samuels, Mike, M.D., and Nancy Samuels. *Seeing with the Mind's Eye.* NY: Random House, 1975.

INDEX

Index